Discovering You

NORTH STAR

Discovering Your North Star

Charting Your Course for Success & Significance

Dr. Dwight "Ike" Reighard
with Pat Springle

FOREWORD BY ZIG ZIGLAR

Copyright © 1998 by Dwight "Ike" Reighard
Quantum Leap Publishing

Published in the United States of America

ISBN: 1-888237-17-1

Photographs by Jimmy Prybil of Friendswood, Texas
Cover design by John Magee of Houston, Texas

Note: Most of the Scripture quotations in this book are from the New International Version. In a few cases, the King James Version is used.

DEDICATION

Just as Polaris, the North Star, is the convergence of three stars, I want to dedicate this book to three stars in my life:

Robin, Danielle, and Abigail.

As captain of our family ship, I am forever indebted to my heaven-sent crew. Robin, my First Officer and best friend, I salute you for 15 wonderful years. We met in a storm and have survived many others. You are a precious gift and the love of my life.

Danielle, you are a wonderful First Mate with your servant's heart. Your commitments will take you far in life. I am honored to be your dad.

Abigail, you are always in our family's Crow's Nest. You look out for all of us, and you protect and defend us with your love. I admire your strength.

At sea, a good captain is willing to go down with his ship, and I'm certainly willing to do anything for you three. It means the world to me to know that each of you, too, would give your lives for one another.

You are stars to me.

TABLE OF CONTENTS

ACKNOWLEDGEMENTS

This book is the result of the encouragement and input of many different people. I want to thank . . .

.... Wade and Trish Pearce and Ernest and Teresa Key for always being there for advice, encouragement, and love.

.... Pam Campbell for editing and proofing the manuscript.

.... Mike Linch and Marlon Longacre for dreaming a dream called NorthStar with me.

.... the people of NorthStar for being such a remarkable family to me. From a dream less than two years ago to the reality today, I am amazed by your commitment to excellence!

.... our Management Team for diving into the deep end of the pool with me! You guys are wonderful!

.... my staff who stepped into the water with me. Together we saw a trickle become a river of fulfillment. Thanks for believing when there was nothing but a dream. You are the best!

FOREWORD

Fact: You will never realize more than a small fraction of your potential as a wandering generality. You must become a meaningful specific. Unfortunately, most people have only a vague idea of what they want, and very few people consistently act on vague ideas. The typical person goes to work every day because that's what he did yesterday. If that's the only reason for going to work today, the odds are long that he will be no more effective today than he was yesterday. The sad thing is, many people who have been with a company five years do not have five years' experience. They have one years' experience five times and no specific plans for making next year anything but a repeat performance.

Harry Emerson Fosdick said it best: "No steam or gas ever drives anything until it is confined. No Niagara is ever turned into light and power until it is tunneled. No life ever grows until it is focused, dedicated, and disciplined."

Hockey superstar Wayne Gretzky brings it clearly into focus when he says, "You will miss 100% of the shots you never take."

Goals work for the individual, the family, a company, and a nation. Goals involve a number of facets. We are making every effort to deal with all of them. A classic example of what happens with this approach is that of Ike Reighard.

Ike was four years old when his family moved from Appalachia to inner-city Atlanta, Georgia. His parents had only completed their educations up to the fifth grade, so when Ike announced that he was going to college, his friends and even some members of his family ridiculed the idea, but Ike was determined to go, and he became the first member of his family to attend college. At the end of his freshman year, he had flunked out big time. Ike spent the next six years as a wandering generality with very little direction in his life. Most of that time he was a disc jockey at a low-powered radio station. He also labored, loading and unloading trucks.

Then one day he picked up a copy of my first book, *See You at the Top*. For the first time in his life, Ike learned that he was a unique individual with remarkable ability, and a brand-new picture of himself was formed. The new Ike started working on one of the new concepts he learned: the importance of having goals. Julius Erving (Dr. J) accurately states that "your goals determine what you're going to be."

Ike's first goal was to go back to college; however, his academic record was so miserable that Mercer University rejected him twice. After the second rejection, Dean Jean Hendrix bumped into him, and Ike poured out his heart to her and shed a few tears in the process. As a result, she permitted him to enroll conditionally. She required him to maintain a B average, or his academic career would be ended again.

A more confident, meaningful, specific, fear-free (well, almost) Ike Reighard had replaced the wandering generality, and he reentered the doors of academia with his goals clearly in mind. By going year-round and taking twenty hours per quarter, two years and three months later he graduated magna cum laude. His goals by then were even higher. That is one of the exciting benefits of having a goals program. As you accomplish your first objectives, new ones are born, your confidence grows, your competence improves, you get more done, and you have more fun in the process.

Today, this child of a pulpwood cutter/stone and quarry worker is Dr. Ike Reighard, pastor of NorthStar Church in Kennesaw, Georgia. Actually, as Ike became successful in his own mind (that is where success always starts), his goals grew, and he changed from being a dreamer to a man who had dreams. That's important. When Alexander the Great had a vision (a dream)—and the vision had him—he conquered the world. When he lost the vision or dream, he couldn't conquer a liquor bottle. When David had a vision, he conquered Goliath; when he lost his vision, he couldn't conquer his own lust.

Another factor involved in Ike Reighard's success story is that with his change of direction and self-image, he started treating every day with respect.

Zig Ziglar

From Zig Ziglar, *Over the Top*, (Thomas Nelson Publishers, Nashville, 1994), pp. 184—186. Used by permission.

Hymn to the North Star
by William Cullen Bryant

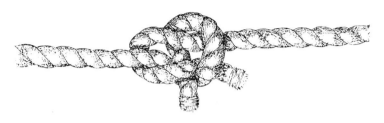

On thy unaltering blaze,
The half-wrecked mariner, his
   compass lost,
Fixes his steady gaze,
And steers, undoubting, to the
   friendly coast;
And they who stray in perilous
   wastes, by night,
Are glad when thou dost shine
   to guide their footsteps right.

1
LOOKING FOR A STAR

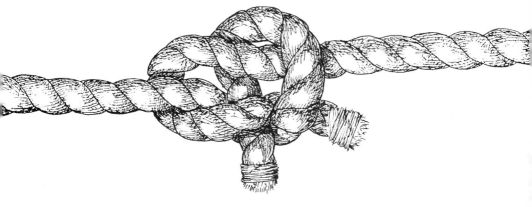

I was at a point of change. No, I was at a point of *crisis*. I had left a successful career months before to take a job that I thought was right for me. It seemed perfect. It seemed like a big step forward. It wasn't. In only a few short months, the new job that had begun with so much promise was unraveling—fast! I had gone there with a clear understanding of my role, but suddenly, several unforeseen events changed that role. For weeks I rode the roller coaster of hoping to resolve the situation but failing time and again. Finally, I faced the cold, hard truth that the dream was dead.

My expectations were shattered. I knew I had to leave, but I had absolutely nowhere to go. I held a job since I was about 11 years old, but now I was cut adrift. I felt lost and alone. I was devastated. What would my peers say? I hoped they wouldn't find out, but I opened the *Atlanta Constitution* the morning after I resigned and saw a blaring, front page story in bold headlines about my departure! Kind of hard to hide now. . . .

It's one thing to fail privately and quietly. It's quite another to fail and have it plastered on the front page of the city newspaper!

Everything I had hoped for was in ruins. That was bad enough, but I felt even worse for Robin and the girls. They had made a big sacrifice to follow me to the new job. Now they had to answer questions like, "Robin, what happened to Ike?" and "Danielle and Abigail, didn't I hear your dad is out of work?" My embarrassment and disillusionment was surpassed only by my fears of how it affected the three people most precious to me.

I decided to get away to spend some time thinking and praying about what to do next with my life. I drove to a cabin in the mountains of Georgia to be alone to think and pray. One night as I sat alone in that cabin, I thought of the story of Abraham. When God called him to leave his home, he didn't know where he was going. Like Abraham almost four millennia ago, I went outside that night and looked up into the stars. I saw the North Star shining in the inky blackness.* Somehow, I knew that star was a symbol for me in my predicament. I needed a new direction. That star was the promise that the guidance I so desperately needed was coming.

That night was a turning point in my life. A new vision began to crystallize. A new plan took shape. Soon, I had a new direction for my career, and with that new direction, my enthusiasm soared.

For generations, navigators have looked to the heavens for guidance. The North Star has provided the most stable reference point in the Northern Hemisphere for people who

---

*Polaris (or North Star) is actually a triple star, the brighter of two visual components being a spectroscopic binary with a period of about 30 years and a Cepheid variable with a period of about 4 days. (*Encyclopedia Britannica*, Volume 9, 1995, p. 556)

have explored the seas and the frontiers. In a world of uncertainty and chaos, it is comforting to know that a single star gives us a reference point so we can find order and purpose.

Each of us needs a North Star which provides security and which does not change. Our individual North Star is a clear sense of purpose which gives us a core set of beliefs, values, and roles. It offers a consistent point of reference for decision-making. This personal North Star enables us to determine what is truly important and to measure our progress in getting where we want to go. We can then focus our efforts instead of trying to wade through so many competing goals. We can say "No" to the distractions, and we can say "Yes" to the things we really value. A lack of focus will keep us mired in the molasses of mediocrity rather than experiencing the empowerment of excellence. Knowing we're on the right track gives us incredible energy to accomplish our dreams. A North Star of personal values also enables us to take responsibility for our own decisions instead of being tossed back and forth by others' expectations and demands.

Having our own personal North Star, then, gives us specific and substantive benefits:
—the security of knowing where we are going,
—core values, purpose, beliefs, and roles,
—a fixed point of reference to always find our way and make mid-course corrections,
—the ability to focus on what is important,
—a bigger "Yes" to things we really value, and
—freedom and responsibility to make our own decisions.

North Star Principles

To keep our focus clear, we need a set of principles which constantly reinforces our values. The North Star Principles, which will be addressed more fully in Chapter

7, encourage us to maintain a vital connection with our sources of strength, hope, and purpose. These principles demand integrity, a commitment to affirming relationships, and high standards of excellence in all we do. The North Star Principles apply to people in every walk of life: the person in busines and the minister, the engineer and the homemaker, the doctor and the janitor. These principles are:

- Embrace risk as a way of life.
- Take responsibility.
- Be honest about your emotions.
- Never stop learning.
- Value meaningful relationships.
- Develop spiritual strength.
- See life as an adventure!

The North Star Principles are a template for setting priorities and making decisions. They are designed to point us back again and again to our deepest motivations and our most compelling sense of purpose. These principles encourage us to stay on course, and they challenge us to go farther and excel still more.

These principles have come out of my own experience and study. Some of them have come fairly easily, but I've learned most of them the hard way! Each one is important in shaping the overall attitude of "objective optimism." If we learn to live by these principles, we will look forward to each day in anticipation of the adventure that awaits us!

Transitions

Change comes easily for some people. In fact, some people invite and create change. Most of us, however, are threatened by change. We may be deeply dissatisfied with our lives, but we gravitate toward the familiar instead of the risky. I've heard people express their fear of the unknown in this way: "This may be hell, but at least I know the names of the streets!"

Most women seem to go through transitions better than men. They reach out to others and find support, perspective, and encouragement. As they mature, the youthful clash of jealous competition for their men gives way to genuine woman-to-woman friendships which continue to deepen over time. Men, on the other hand, often isolate themselves during times of stress and transition. In contrast to women, men's competitive nature continues and even hardens, pushing people away and leaving them feeling alone and desperate. In times of stress and change, they paradoxically become both isolated and dependent at the same time. They want and need help from others, but they are too stubborn or prideful to ask for it. Men can easily get stuck in dead-end lifestyles from which they see no way out. They simmer with anger, becoming numb and listless. It is vitally important that men and women find true purpose in those times of transition—a guiding vision that keeps them energized, focused, connected, and alive.

Finding your North Star may not be easy, and it may not happen quickly, but any amount of effort is worth it! This book is designed to give you insights and encouragement toward this discovery process, but the most important part will be your own reflection and application. This painstaking process of self-discovery may well be more important than any set of goals you set at the end. It determines your character, and a refined character is more valuable than gold. This journey will take you through the deep waters of motivation and desire, and you will be tested by the fire of honest analysis, changed forever, irrevocably and beneficially. Ease, comfort, pleasure, and wealth may be welcome companions from time to time, but they make lousy spouses.

All of us are in the open sea of life. We simply can't stay tied up to the dock. We may want to, but that's not what gives us meaning and purpose. On the open water, we need a strong rudder and tiller of values or we'll be driven by the winds and waves of others' demands or empty despair. None of us wants to be shipwrecked on "Gilligan's Island"! We desperately need a clear course heading and a strong ship to get us there. God wants us to experience "the abundant life." Some of us may define this abundant life as the acquisition of money and possessions, but it means far more than that. Abundance is found in living for a cause greater than ourselves and in relationships that are honest and intimate. We must not settle for anything less! Psychologist Abraham Maslow said, "The story of the human race is men and women selling themselves short." Solomon, the king of Israel, said it in a different way: "Without vision, the people perish" (Proverbs 29:18).

Please don't misunderstand me. I'm not advocating headlong pursuit of a wild-eyed, irrational dream that only takes us farther away from real meaning and purpose. Most of us risk too little and settle for mediocrity, but a few of us take inordinate risks. The damage from irrational pursuits is just as bad (or worse) than not trying at all. In the words of that renowned, modern philosopher, Dirty Harry, "A man's got to know his limitations."

The Necessity of Reflection

I have a few books I go back to time after time to refresh my spirit and my dreams. I hope this book will do that for you. Parts of it will be fun to read, and some of the exercises will be encouraging, but you will probably find a place or two that challenges some of your most cherished dreams and shakes your sense of security. Reading, studying, reflecting, and applying the principles in these pages will give you a clear sense of direction for every aspect of your life.

One of the great ironies I have observed is that young couples spend thousands of dollars (and sometimes tens of thousands of dollars) on a wedding, but they balk when I suggest that they go through pre-marital counseling. They are unwilling to spend a few hundred dollars to learn the personality and temperament of their soon-to-be spouse so their marriage and their relationship with their children will be based on clear understanding and wisdom. They are more than willing to spend piles of dollars on flowers, food, a band, hotel rooms, and pictures—all for a three-hour event—but they are unwilling to spend a small fraction of that for an experience that could provide a firm foundation for rich relationships for the rest of their lives. In the same way, people spend weeks and thousands of dollars planning their dream vacations, but when it's over, they walk back into the same old house and go to the same old jobs with the same old feelings that life is dull and boring. They plan and dream for that vacation, but strangely, they have few if any plans and dreams for their lives. Many of us have never been given the opportunity to plan and dream in a way that makes sense.

This book uncovers the (perhaps hidden) pattern of success in your life and points you toward your greatest potential in every important area. It will help you understand how those with your personality dream and plan most effectively. And in these pages, you will be challenged to rethink what you hold dear. You may just find that the things others told you to value aren't that important to you, or you may find an old dream being rekindled.

We're all headed somewhere, whether we know where that destination is or not, and whether we want to go there or not. I'd much rather pour my energies and time into people and goals that I've decided are the most important things in the world. Then one day I can look back on my life and have no regrets. We all experience roadblocks and detours in our families, our jobs, and our health, but if we don't have a clear idea where we want to go, every road-block and detour becomes a crisis instead of a challenge.

We're not alone in this process. Most of us can find trustworthy friends who will encourage us to keep looking to the heavens until we find our North Star. We sure don't want to be around people who tell us to quit or who say any old star will do! But we have someone even greater to help us: the Creator of those stars. God graciously waits for each and every one of us to look to Him for guidance. Solomon told us, "Trust in the Lord with all your heart and lean not on your own understanding; in all your ways acknowledge him, and he will make your paths straight" (Proverbs 3:5-6 NIV). People lean on their own understanding all the time, and it gets them into trouble! We think we know the right thing to do, the right motivations, and the right way to treat people, but we desperately need the Designer to give us guidance so our lives are not an endless series of dead ends and detours. Some of us think that God is a cosmic kill-joy, ready to slap us down if He sees us having fun or being successful, but God isn't that way at all. He has proven His great love when Jesus Christ paid the supreme price for us. He's crazy about us! And He wants us to enjoy life to the fullest . . . and that means in a rich, real, relationship with Him so He can give us the encouragement and direction we need. When we are connected to Him, we tap into the creative forces that made the stars themselves! A friend of mine talks about "getting into the Gulf Stream of God's

Spirit." We no longer are left to our own energies. God Himself moves us along and adds His enormous power to our efforts. When we trust in Him with all our hearts, He moves mountains, opens doors, and shuts the mouths of lions. Oh, we'll still go through a desert from time to time, but never alone. He's the one who hung the North Star in the heavens, and He's the one who wants each of us to find our own personal North Star of love, success, and fulfillment.

I hope you will make a commitment to read every word in this book and take every step that you need to take. Discovering your North Star is one of the most awesome journeys you will ever take, so determine now not to turn back. Don't live your life by default. Discover your North Star, pursue your dreams, and accelerate your potential in every area of your life.

Read the following statement. If you are willing to make that commitment, sign and date it.

Today, I make a firm commitment to pursue my North Star so my life and my relationships will have more depth, meaning, and purpose. I will read every page of this book, work through every exercise, and take every step that is right for me.

Name   Date

Self-fulfilling Prophecy

Attitude makes all the difference. You may have heard the story of the identical twins who looked so much alike their own parents had a hard time telling them apart— except that one was an undying optimist and the other was a cynical pessimist. Their father tried to help each of them find more balance in their perspectives, but nothing worked. The optimistic child always saw good in every situation, and the pessimist unfailingly found negatives in every circumstance. The father took the twins to a child psychologist to find some answers. The psychologist examined the twins very carefully, then he gave his advice: "Christmas will be here soon. I want you to give your pessimistic child absolutely anything he mentions. No matter what it is, get it for him. And your optimistic child? Don't give him anything. On second thought, go by the horse stable and clean out one of the stalls. Put it in a box and wrap it up. Then give it to your optimistic son on Christmas morning. Do these things, and you'll bring balance to your twins."

On Christmas morning, the twins came downstairs and found dozens of wrapped packages under the tree. The father began giving present after present to the pessimistic child. As he opened each one, he whined, "It's the wrong color! It's the wrong size! It's not exactly what I wanted!"

Finally, only one box remained. The father took it over to the optimistic child (who had been waiting so patiently) and handed it to him. The beaming child ripped off the paper, tore open the box, and looked inside. At that moment, the boy laughed and screamed and hollered! He ran up and down the stairs and all over the house. The father was dumbfounded. He shook his head, thinking, *I've warped him! I've ruined him! He's gone crazy!*

The father tried to stop the boy to calm him down, but the little boy wouldn't stop. The father soberly reminded him, "Son, didn't you see what was in the box?"

The boy looked at him and exclaimed, "Yeah, Dad. Isn't it great?! There's got to be a pony around here some place!"

Some of us, like the pessimistic child, can't seem to find anything good no matter what gifts we receive. But some of us have the incredible ability to look in the box that life has given us and our conclusion is: There must be a pony around here some place!

There's a lot to be said for "self-fulfilling prophecy." A person's outlook usually determines the unfolding of events—and it certainly makes a difference in whether life is exciting and fun or tense and dull. As you go through the journey of discovering your North Star, remember: attitude makes all the difference.

❑ Reflect on each of the North Star Principles. Write a progress report for each one. (In what ways are you excelling? In what ways do you need to see changes?)

—Embrace risk as a way of life.

—Take responsibility.

—Be honest about your emotions.

—Never stop learning.

—Value meaningful relationships.

—Develop spiritual strength.

—See life as an adventure!

❑ Which of these seem most attractive to you? Explain:

❑ Which are most threatening to you? Explain:

❑ What do you hope to get out of reading this book and reflecting on the exercises and questions?

2
DEATH BY INCHES

Nobody wakes up in the morning and decides to have a boring, dead-end life—but it happens. The dreams we cherished as young adults sometimes become only faded memories. The enthusiasm that used to energize us erodes and vanishes. Our once-taut muscles are now knots of tension. What happened? What went wrong?

Death by inches is the slow, gradual accumulation of the heat and pressures of life without making needed changes. We let circumstances dictate our direction, and we take the path of least resistance instead of seizing the challenges and making sure we stay on track. Most of us can't identify a dividing line between the time we had that driving purpose and the time we lost it. The change happened much too gradually. We can tell if we've experienced death by inches when:

- We almost always take the safe way and are unwilling to take risks.
- We go to work to pay the bills and live for vacations.
- We think of work when we're home and think of home when we're at work.

- Nothing excites us.
- Most of life is just going through the motions with no purpose.
- Our thoughts are consumed with trivial "have to's."
- We avoid decisions.
- We blame others for our misfortunes.
- We daydream about retirement (even though it's many years away).
- We gripe about the specifics of our ill health far too much.
- We live in and through our children, and we have no life of our own.
- We can't sleep, or we sleep too much.
- We eat the same things at the same places with the same people, and talk about the same things day after day, week after week, month after month.
- We are almost always grouchy.
- We withdraw in discouragement or explode in rage . . . or both.
- We get involved in really dumb behavior that hurts us and others, and we won't or can't change.
- We talk a lot about what "we used to do."
- There's nothing we really enjoy or that brings us pleasure.
- Promotions, moves, deaths, betrayals, and health all seem to be out of our control.
- Our thoughts are filled with regrets and "if onlys":
    If only I'd studied when I was in school. . . .
    If only I'd taken that job. . . .
    If only I'd married somebody else. . . .
    If only I'd made more money. . . .
    If only I'd had better parents. . . .
    If only I hadn't blown it so badly. . . .
    If only everybody hadn't been against me. . . .
    If only I knew what to do. . . .
    If only I was free to do what I wanted to do. . . .

The Causes of a Dead-end Life

Stagnation in our lives and careers can be caused by any of a multitude of factors that often come in clusters. If they happened one at a time, we could identify them more clearly and deal with them more effectively, but when several occur at the same time, we get overwhelmed. For example, young couples often have to juggle buying a house, having children, moving, and job stresses all at the same time. Middle-age adults have the common stresses of raising teenagers, sending them off to college, paying for that college education, caring for aging parents, the threat of downsizing at work, and personal health concerns. Combinations of disappointments and stresses steal our vision and erode our enthusiasm. Here are some of the most common—and the most devastating—causes of death by inches:

—a strained marriage which consumes our mental and emotional energies

—career disappointments, a belligerent boss, and unrealistic expectations at work

—children who are out of control

—severe or chronic health problems in the immediate family

—severe financial problems

—dealing with a family member who has severe emotional or psychological problems, such as alcoholism

—the corrosive effects of bitterness

—the shame of past, unresolved failures

Gradually, these things (and many others) blur our dreams until they no longer exist. We don't think any more about making a difference. We only want to make it through the day. Our lofty goals and expectations are lowered with each passing disappointment, each passing dull day. We become self-focused and intense about our own well-being, or worse, we become apathetic altogether. I have listened to people talk about their experience of losing passion for life and settling for a dull existence. Their words sound a lot like the classic line in *Cat on a Hot Tin Roof*. Brick, the withdrawn husband in Tennessee Williams' play, never got over the fact that all of life wasn't like that wonderful, shining moment when he scored his famous touchdown. "Why," he asks for all of us, "can't it always be that good?"

People who have lost purpose and passion say things like:

- "I'm never able to do what I want to do."
- "I feel smothered by her."
- "I feel so tied down. I wish I could be free."
- "How did I get so much responsibility and so little help and time?"
- "Nothing is ever going to change."
- "My life is out of control, and there's nothing I can do about it."
- "I feel hopeless. I don't even know how to take the first step."
- "I'm doing all I know to do, but it isn't enough. I'm falling farther behind every day."
- "I wish I could go back and make different decisions. There's nothing I can do about them now."
- "I need to find out who I really am." (When I hear that, I want to say, "Hey, look at your driver's license! That might give you a clue!" But I usually keep my mouth shut.)

As I have observed people go through these stresses, I have seen one factor that robs us of positive passion more than any other: bitterness. Oh, there's plenty of passion in bitterness. In fact, it provides tremendous energy, but it is the destructive energy of a tornado, not the constructive energy of a power plant. The writer to the Hebrews instructed us, "See to it that . . . no bitter root grows up to cause trouble and defile many" (Hebrews 12:15). The Greek word for *root* refers to a particular type of root that is taken from the ground, dried, ground up, and mixed with oil or water. It was then used as a dye or stain. So what this verse means is: Be careful not to let bitterness take over your life because it will color how you look at the world, and it will stain every relationship, goal, and thought. Bitterness leads to cynicism so that people question any kindness they receive and every gentle word they hear uttered. People whose lives are stained by bitterness push others away. They despise other people and, in truth, they despise themselves.

Bitterness stains a person's very identity. He identifies himself as "the one who was wronged." The person's role becomes "the avenger" instead of loving parent, grateful child, or pleasant and effective employee. Bitter people are demanding people. They demand that others suffer for the offensive behavior they inflict. They expect every person they meet to fill the gaping hole (created by the wrong) by loving them, giving to them, protecting them, and comforting them. Of course, these people don't have a clue they have to make up for others' wrongs, so they are blindsided by these demands. And bitter people are adamant that they won't ever be hurt again. Of course, that expectation is totally unreasonable. All of us, if we are in relationships and live in the real world, experience hurt from time to time. The bitter person can't "roll with the punches" or forgive. Each new offense, no matter how slight, is perceived as another grievous wound, and the demands only multiply and harden. Not a pretty picture, but a very common one. I once knew a bitter man who owned a farm with a beautiful, fishing lake. His neighbor said, "The greatest joy he gets out of the lake is telling others they can't fish there."

Our personality makes a difference in how we experience death by inches. A strong, decisive person becomes harsh and belligerent. An enthusiastic, energetic person loses zeal for life and becomes dull and bored. A sensitive, loyal person withdraws into the relative safety of loneliness. And a structured, detailed person loses himself or herself in the myriad intricacies and demands of her work. In different individuals, death by inches may take the form of:

—a volcano, simmering quietly until pressure builds and it explodes

—a zombie, emotionless and apathetic, giving up on love and meaning

—a wallflower, afraid of being hurt again, unwilling to take risks

—a critic, finding fault in anything and everything

—a Pollyanna, always pleasant, always shallow

—a clown, covering the emptiness and pain with a few laughs

—a fixer, unable to solve his own problems, so he focuses on others' problems

—a marionette, dancing any time someone pulls its string

It takes tremendous courage to face the facts in our lives if we have experienced death by inches. If it had happened all at once, we could grab the dragon by the throat and slay it! But the accumulation of multiple stresses, the breakdown of important relationships, the disappointments piling up day after day, and the corrosion of bitterness all take their toll. It is easier to close our eyes and just keep going the way we are going. In his book, *Lincoln on Leadership*, Donald Phillips relates a story about the president. At one point during the Civil War, Lincoln's cabinet told him they had good reason to believe that many who they had thought were patriots were actually Southern spies.

Lincoln valued loyalty above all else, and it distressed him deeply to hear about trusted friends whose fidelity was now in question. After presenting a large and condemning body of evidence, Secretary of War Stanton asked Lincoln for direction on how to deal with the problem. In reply, a visibly upset Lincoln told this story about a farmer who had a very large tree next to his house:

> It was a majestic-looking tree, and apparently perfect in every part—tall, straight, and of immense size—the grand old sentinel of his forest home. One morning, while at work in his garden, he saw a squirrel [run up the tree into a hole] and thought the tree might be hollow. He proceeded to examine it carefully and, much to his surprise, he found that the stately [tree] that he had [valued] for its beauty and grandeur to be the pride and protection of his little farm was hollow from top to bottom. Only a rim of sound wood remained, barely sufficient to support its weight. What was he to do? If he cut it down, it would [do great damage] with its length and spreading branches. If he let it remain, his family was in constant danger. In a storm it might fall, or the wind might blow it down, and his house and children be crushed by it. What should he do? As he turned away, he said sadly: "I wish I had never seen that squirrel."[1]

There are times in our lives when we are hollow on the inside, and the easiest thing to do is to try to ignore the squirrel. The wisest thing to do is to examine the truth and embrace it. That's the only way we can make wise and effective changes.

Listen to what people say when you ask, "How are you doing?" You'll hear enthusiastic remarks like:
- "I'm getting by."
- "Doing OK, I guess."
- "Fine" . . . which means: Don't ask for an explanation.
- "All right, under the circumstances."
- "Hanging in there."

A lot of people have a rocking chair mentality: a lot of motion with no progress. They are like the plate spinner on the old "Ed Sullivan Show" who rushed around to the music of "Flight of the Bumble Bee," spinning plate after plate to keep all of them in the air until he got the last one going. A lot of activity, but very little accomplishment. Some of us are doing the same thing—running to work, taking kids to practice, shopping, going to parties, church, and all kinds of other events, hoping we can keep it all going and it all doesn't crash. The only thing we need is the soundtrack to "Flight of the Bumble Bee"!

And our children are watching, ready to take our places as plate spinners. I'm convinced we are much too busy today. The Bible calls it "worldliness," letting ourselves be squeezed into the values and lifestyles the world thinks are important. We need to stop spinning some of those plates and refocus on the things that are really important. Even God took a day off! And He designed the Sabbath so we can take a deep breath and rest as well. Then we can regain perspective. Then we can be recharged. But genuine rest is not just a once-a-week thing. It comes from the absence of inner conflicts as we throw out the extraneous that competes with the important, and throwing out some of the important because they compete with the absolutely crucial.

On fall afternoons, I like to watch football. One of the things that frustrates me the most is the "prevent defense." Years ago, Georgia played Alabama in one of their classic, herculean contests. The game was hard fought. There were great plays on both sides. With only a couple of minutes to go in the game, Georgia led by about four points. Alabama had the ball, and Georgia went into the prevent defense. The Alabama quarterback threw 20 yard pass after 20 yard pass under the Georgia safeties, and in only four plays, Alabama scored and went ahead. Georgia took the kickoff, and Alabama went into their prevent defense. Georgia threw passes underneath the Alabama Crimson Tide safeties, and the Bulldogs scored in only five plays. With only seconds left in the game, Alabama got the ball one last time. They had time for a couple of plays, so Georgia put its safeties way down field. The first play went for about 40 yards, and on the last play of the game, the Alabama wide receiver caught the ball at about the 10 yard line and ran it in to win the game.

Prevent defenses allow momentum to shift very widely and very quickly. The focus shifts from trying to win the game to avoiding losing it. The team no longer is aggressive and intent on stopping the other team. Instead they are willing to give up large chunks of yardage in the hope that they won't give up too much. When you have momentum, you appear to be a lot better than you really are. And when you lose momentum, you aren't nearly as bad as you appear. Momentum is very important in football . . . and in life. The prevent defense is designed to keep from losing, not to win the game. Many of us have the same personal philosophy. Our objective is to keep from losing, so we give up on lots of goals, plans, and dreams and try to hang on to a few things to show for our efforts. The end result is that we inevitably give up far too much, and we (like the Bulldogs on that day) are left feeling empty and angry.

Sometimes we get off course and we never get turned around. Several years ago, a young football coach named

Bo Rein had just accepted the prestigious job of being the head coach at LSU. He was on a recruiting trip, flying in a private jet to visit some top high school prospects. No one knows what happened that day. The plane passed its destination and continued flying . . . and continued flying. Airfields along the route tried to contact the plane, but none of the calls to the pilot were answered. Air Force jets were dispatched to chase the plane. When they caught up to it and flew alongside, they saw no signs of life in the cockpit. The plane was obviously on autopilot on a particular heading. Rein and the pilot continued out to sea and finally crashed. Author Gordon McDonald noted that if people had seen the young, successful football coach and an experienced pilot get into that private jet that morning, they would have thought these two men were on top of the world. They were flying high and fast. But there was an internal malfunction on that plane. On the outside, they appeared to have it all together, but on the inside, something was terribly wrong . . . and it led to death.

The Titanic sank because what was on the outside got on the inside. In the same way, people can withstand almost anything as long as they have perspective and can keep the poison of despair outside their hearts. When that poison gets in, it colors every thought, action, goal, and relationship. I heard a very successful man say one day, "I'm trying to work myself into a heart attack." The stresses in his life were so great that he concluded the best way out was to die in flaming glory, to let life end in heart failure because he worked himself to death. At least then he could say he did it for his family or his company. To him, it was the honorable way out. And there are a lot of other people just like this man who want to be carried out on their shield. Their pall bearers can say, "He never took a vacation. He was so committed to his work. What an example!" Indeed.

Many of us abdicate our dreams to others. We do what they want us to do, we go where they want us to go, we think what they want us to think, and we dream only what they allow us to dream. Psychologists speak of the stark difference between an "internal locus of control" and an "external locus of control." An external locus of control means we let others determine the path and quality of our lives. We are like puppets or marionettes. Other people pull our strings, and we dance. Some of us are so fearful we have learned to "read" even the slightest change in others' tone of voice or the most subtle raising of an eyebrow. We instantly change to win their approval or stave off their rejection. We may gladly abdicate our freedom and identities because we are afraid of making our own decisions or because we hope the other person is loving and wise enough to know what's best for us. But sooner or later, we resent the control—even though we desperately want it so we don't have the responsibility of making our own decisions. At that point, bitterness is mixed with fear.

Making our own decisions—having an internal locus of control—is very threatening to some of us, especially if we have let others make decisions for us for decades. But taking responsibility for our own hopes and dreams—and yes, our own failures and heartaches—gives us tremendous freedom and strength.

I know a man who grew up in an alcoholic home. His mother was the one who ruled the household while his dad drank and moved from job to job. The mother felt out of control in relation to her husband, but she was determined not to be out of control in relation to her son! She told him what to wear, how to eat, who to spend time with, and every other decision about his life. And it didn't end when he went to college. She continued to try to rule his life . . . and she succeeded. His mother's smothering control robbed this man of his sense of freedom and competence. He felt that he couldn't make decisions on his own. Why? Because every time he did, he was pushed back into place with condemnation and criticism of his controlling mother. He learned not to trust himself, and he learned to only do what others told him to do. Now, don't get me wrong. This guy wasn't a wallflower. He became a successful executive, but he was successful because he was absolutely driven to do what his bosses wanted done. He was, in some ways, the ideal employee . . . except that he was dying inside. He had job-competence, but not self-confidence. He knew he could perform tasks, but he never believed he had a life of his own—and he didn't. He was only an extension of what his mother wanted, then what his bosses wanted, and then what his wife wanted. He finally came to a point that he knew he had to change. This man went through the process of learning to take control of his life, making his own decisions, and not feeling he had to please everybody in every way. It has been a difficult journey, but one that is paying off in peace, honesty, and freedom.

Many of us work hard for years in the hope that we can be comfortable and relaxed in retirement. We see commercials about happy older couples rowing boats in serene waters while the announcer tells us that they made wise investments. It looks pretty good—especially if we're working 60 to 80 hours a week to afford our kids' college education and still put a little in our 401(k)! But there are two things wrong with this picture: First, many of us are forfeiting our present for our future. We need to live in the now. Our spouses, children, and co-workers—even ourselves—will benefit far more from us enjoying life along the way instead of killing ourselves (in some cases, literally) so we can be comfortable at the end of our lives. The second thing wrong with that picture of retirement is that we don't need to turn off our ambition, energy, and creativity when we reach the age of 65. Certainly, that age can spell a time of transition, but the change doesn't have to be from workaholism to lethargy. We can alter our focus from earning to leaving a legacy, from getting to giving, from looking at our watches to looking at eternity. Many people tell me that the absence of purpose after retirement kills as quickly as any disease.

Change is sometimes welcome, sometimes threatening, but inevitable in each of our lives. We can try to avoid it at all costs, but then we lose all the joy of seeing dreams fulfilled. The key is to *create* change when possible and to *respond appropriately* to change when necessary. Too many of us are experiencing death by inches. We can arrest that process now! Today!

❑ Are you dying by inches? On a scale of 0 (not at all) to 10 (all day, every day), rate your experience of these symptoms of dying by inches:

—I almost always take the safe way and am unwilling to take risks.

0   1   2   3   4   5   6   7   8   9   10

—I go to work to pay the bills and live for vacations.

0   1   2   3   4   5   6   7   8   9   10

—I think of work when I'm home and think of home when I'm at work.

0   1   2   3   4   5   6   7   8   9   10

—Nothing excites me.

0 1 2 3 4 5 6 7 8 9 10

—Most of life is just going through the motions with no purpose.

0 1 2 3 4 5 6 7 8 9 10

—My thoughts are consumed with trivial "have to's."

0 1 2 3 4 5 6 7 8 9 10

—I avoid decisions.

0 1 2 3 4 5 6 7 8 9 10

—I blame others for my misfortunes.

0 1 2 3 4 5 6 7 8 9 10

—I gripe about the specifics of my ill health far too much.

0 1 2 3 4 5 6 7 8 9 10

—I live in and through my children and have no life of my own.

0 1 2 3 4 5 6 7 8 9 10

—I can't sleep, or I sleep too much.

0 1 2 3 4 5 6 7 8 9 10

—I eat the same things at the same places with the same people, and talk about the same things day after day, week after week, month after month.

0 1 2 3 4 5 6 7 8 9 10

—I am almost always grouchy.

0   1   2   3   4   5   6   7   8   9   10

—I withdraw in discouragement or explode in rage . . . or both.

0   1   2   3   4   5   6   7   8   9   10

—I get involved in really dumb behavior that hurts me and others, and I won't or can't change.

0   1   2   3   4   5   6   7   8   9   10

—I talk a lot about what "I used to do."

0   1   2   3   4   5   6   7   8   9   10

—There's nothing I really enjoy or take pleasure in.

0   1   2   3   4   5   6   7   8   9   10

—Promotions, moves, deaths, betrayals, and health all seem to be out of my control.

0   1   2   3   4   5   6   7   8   9   10

❏ Put a check next to those "if onlys" you feel:

___If only I'd studied when I was in school. . . .

___If only I'd taken that job. . . .

___If only I'd married somebody else. . . .

___If only I made more money. . . .

___If only I'd had better parents. . . .

___If only I hadn't blown it so bad. . . .

___If only everybody hadn't been against me. . . .

___If only I knew what to do. . . .

___If only I was free to do what I wanted to do. . . .

❏ List the most significant stresses you have experienced in the past five years.

❏ Have these stolen your passion and eroded your dreams, or have they focused your priorities and sharpened your desires and plans? Explain:

❏ What effects have you seen bitterness have on other people's lives? (relationships, health, attitude, etc.)

❏ Is there someone you need to forgive in order to break the pattern of bitterness?

❏ Think of those closest to you. How does each one respond to stress? Write their names next to the pattern that fits best:

—a rock, cool, calm, and reasonable

—a volcano, simmering quietly until the pressure builds and it explodes

—a zombie, emotionless and apathetic, giving up on love and meaning

—a wallflower, afraid of being hurt again, unwilling to take risks

—a critic, finding fault in anything and everything

—a Pollyanna, always pleasant, always shallow

—a clown, covering the emptiness with a few laughs

—a fixer, unable to solve his own problems, so he focuses on others' problems

—a puppet, always doing what others want

❏ Which pattern best fits your response? Explain:

❏ What does it mean to "live not to lose" instead of "living to win"?

❑ Look back at the North Star Principles in Chapter 1. How would following these principles help you overcome any tendencies to experience death by inches in your life?

❑ What are three things you can do to begin to really live?

3
DEAD RECKONING

To chart his course to his destination, a navigator first needs to know his present position. *Dead reckoning* is the calculation of the position of a ship through an analysis of previous entries in the ship's log. In other words, it is a study of the past in order to chart a course for the future. The same process can be applied to our lives so we can achieve more success than we ever thought possible.

Success is defined in many different ways. For some, success is achieving great goals; for others, it is establishing order and structure to any project; others feel good when they have done a lot of research and found new insights to an old problem; and still others feel successful when they develop meaningful relationships. It is often very instructive to look back and see the pattern of success we have experienced in our lives. As we analyze the things we have enjoyed over the years, our own, unique template of success becomes clear. The patterns of the past then become a foundation for the future.

I took the time to look back at my life to see the pattern of success and fulfillment. Here's what I found.

I can remember having friends from my earliest years. On the first day I walked into kindergarten, I had buddies. Having friends and being a friend has always been easy for me. Good relationships with people have always provided richness and meaning to my life.

I also enjoyed going to school and learning about new things. I wasn't driven by the goal of making good grades (my mother will tell you that!) and, to be honest, I didn't take tests all that well. But I loved to learn and read. I grew up during the early days of space exploration, watching Shepherd, Grissom, and Glenn blast off into space. I just knew I'd be an astronaut some day. Astronomy fascinated me because I wondered what might be out there, but history intrigued me when I discovered the drama of actual events. I loved studying about the men who lived and led during the Civil War. Many of these men, like Stonewall Jackson and Abraham Lincoln, overcame great obstacles to become incredible leaders. Overcomers have always fascinated me, partly because of my personality and temperament, and partly because of my own parents. They both attended school only as far as the fifth grade, but they were avid readers who learned for a lifetime. They always encouraged me to read. By the time we moved to Atlanta when I was four years old, I was a big fan of the local bookmobile. The lady who drove it to our neighborhood told me, "Ike, you need to develop your love for reading, because you'll be able to go places in books that you can't go any other way." She instilled in me a deep desire to read. I devoured the *Weekly Reader* in school. My parents bought the 1955 *Funk and Wagnall's Encyclopedia*. Whenever I had a few minutes, I pulled those big brown hardback volumes off the shelf and read about all kinds of interesting things. I couldn't get enough! From those earliest days, I had a sense of awe about people, events, and nature. When I read, I was an explorer on a journey to new, exciting places with new, exciting people. Charlie "Tremendous" Jones, motivational speaker and author of *Life is Tremendous!*, observed, "The books I read and the people I meet change me more than anything else." Me, too, Charlie!

As an adult, I have enjoyed building up people and seeing them succeed. Everybody needs someone to believe in them, but some of us hear very few voices of encouragement. I want to be that voice for others. I enjoy seeing the potential in people—which they may not even see themselves—and it thrills me to help them discover the potential and find purpose, success, and rich relationships. I move toward people who seem to struggle and need some help. Really good teachers believe there's never been a bad kid. I agree. I don't believe there are worthless people anywhere. They just need someone to come alongside and help them unlock their potential so they can maximize their lives. I'm not talking just about finances. That's important, but other parts of life are equally or more important. As I encourage people, they encourage me in return. Zig Ziglar says that if we help enough people achieve their goals, they'll help us achieve ours. That's the old principle of sowing and reaping.

A friend of mine noticed that I talk often about building up people, but seldom about building organizations—even though I am involved in several organizations as a leader and board member. My focus is on individuals. I seldom even think of the organizations. Somehow, this focus has been successful because I encourage many of these individuals, who are more goal-oriented and interested in building up their organizations than I am, to get involved and create the structure. Organizations and companies certainly need time and attention, but I get a kick out of helping individual men and women discover and achieve their dreams. That's what turns me on. Some people may see this as a flaw in my leadership, but as long as I value other people's organizational skills, the full range of goals are accomplished. If I focused on organizational goals, not only would I be miserable, I'd make other people miserable, too! We're all happier when we do what we do best and when we focus on what gives us the greatest sense of fulfillment . . . without neglecting the important contributions of people who have differing gifts and skills.

Years ago I dreamed of creating a church which would be known for healing the hurts of "broken world people." We would be a group of people who gently restore those whose lives are battered and bleeding, and a lot of people who had lost hope and direction would find both by being with us. Our church would be compassion focused. When I went through my difficult transition of leaving one job and having nowhere to go, I found the path to fulfill that dream. I'm living that dream now, and it is so fulfilling I can hardly stand it!

As we dream and plan for the future, it is instructive to look back and see the pattern of success in our past. The exercises in this chapter will help you uncover that pattern. Remember, people define success very differently. Think about those times when you felt particularly fulfilled, when you enjoyed achieving a goal or helping a person. Take plenty of time to reflect. Some memories will come very quickly, but if you are patient, events and people may come to mind that you haven't thought of for years. Don't try to fit the memories together—at least not yet. Just let them come. Write them down and stay open to any memories that surface. As an example, I have given you *my memories* of past successes in the opening paragraphs of this chapter.

❏ For each period of your childhood and adolescence, identify at least two or three examples when you succeeded in and enjoyed an activity. Write a brief description of each instance. (For example, you may have built a model airplane, made a dress with your mom, hosted a party, excelled in a sport, made good grades, led a group at school, conducted a treasure hunt, planned a family event, achieved merit badges in Scouting, won an award for something, started your own business, made the cheerleading squad, learned to play a musical instrument, etc.)

Childhood (5-9)
1.

2.

3.

Pre-Teen Years (10-12)
1.

2.

3.

Adolescence (13-18)
1.

2.

3.

❏ List and describe at least ten instances in your adult life in which you succeeded in an activity and enjoyed it. (For example, you may have received a commendation at work, learned a new hobby or skill, designed and built something yourself, received an award, climbed a mountain, been elected to a position in a club, formed a close group of friends, helped someone out of an addiction, mentored someone, designed a new system at work that saved the company a lot of money, planned a great vacation for your family, written a book, etc.)

1.

2.

3.

4.

5.

6.

7.

8.

9.

10.

❑ Examine the entire list from childhood, teenage years, and adulthood. Which six events stand out as most significant to you? Write a detailed description of each event:

1. Event:
How and why did you choose to do this activity?

Explain how you did it:

What about this event was meaningful to you? Why?

2. Event:
How and why did you choose to do this activity?

Explain how you did it:

What about this event was meaningful to you? Why?

3. Event:

How and why did you choose to do this activity?

Explain how you did it:

What about this event was meaningful to you? Why?

4. Event:

How and why did you choose to do this activity?

Explain how you did it:

What about this event was meaningful to you? Why?

5. Event:
How and why did you choose to do this activity?

Explain how you did it:

What about this event was meaningful to you? Why?

6. Event:
How and why did you choose to do this activity?

Explain how you did it:

What about this event was meaningful to you? Why?

❑ Go back over your descriptions of the six events and circle the words which are significant to you (words which describe your feelings, your specific contributions, your relationships, the types of activities, etc.).
List those words here:

As I examined what I enjoy doing and what I have done well, several words came to mind: vision, building, teaching, encouraging, serving. Some other words definitely didn't come to mind: organizing, enforcing, monitoring. Those aren't wrong. They just aren't me!

❑ What strengths show up consistently in your successes? Circle all that apply:

serving	leading	helping
planning	organizing	directing
evaluating	calculating	building
teaching	researching	investigating
understanding	acting	creating
assembling	writing	painting
speaking	finishing	taking initiative
selling	achieving	monitoring
quantifying	encouraging	innovating
motivating	competing	producing
controlling	enforcing	fine-tuning
persuading	managing	problem solving

❏ Go back over the list of strengths and draw a line through those that are definitely not strengths of yours.

❏ Describe your motivations in these times of success and enjoyment. (What has "revved your engines"? What kept you up nights excitedly thinking and planning? What has made you smile and feel a deep sense of satisfaction?)

What pattern(s) do you see in your motivations?

❏ Write a detailed analysis of your past successes:
I have consistently seen success in these types of activities:

When I am successful, I feel:

When I am successful, my relationships with others are characterized by:

I am energized and motivated by seeing potential in people and the vision of how I can help them be successful in every area of their lives. I love to help people. In some ways, I would have enjoyed being a coach (and to tell the truth, that's exactly what I'm doing now!).

The things that hinder me in fulfilling my dreams are procrastination and discouragement. I am energized by people, and it's hard for me to knuckle down and be disciplined enough to do detail work. It's easier to put it off. I'm a visionary, and I tend to get bogged down in details. Some people enjoy checking things off their lists of things to do. I don't even like to make a list! I like to initiate an idea, find good people to participate, and even raise the money for it, but please don't give me a four page "to do" list!

I get discouraged when people don't see in themselves what I see. Negative people are a drain to me. When I'm around people who find fault in everybody and everything, I can feel my enthusiasm dwindle away, and I really have to concentrate on staying positive (or getting away from them).

I don't mind people who are cynical but are trying hard to be more positive. I am thrilled when people want to change in that way. But it drives me crazy to be around people who try to intimidate others with their anger and griping so they can get others to do whatever they want.

Life is hard enough without having other people be a constant drain on us. Some people try to control us instead of respecting us enough to treat us like adults. My friend, nationally-known expert on leadership, John Maxwell, made this observation: "It is very difficult to run through a minefield by yourself. And it is almost impossible to do it when you are handcuffed to somebody else!" People who drag us down are real obstacles to our growth and progress.

❏ When I am successful, the obstacles I often overcome are:

I am thrilled when I can be involved in motivating people to make specific, concrete steps in their lives. Speaking, counseling, studying, and helping people . . . that's what I love to do!

❏ The activities I have most enjoyed in my life are:

Everything has a price tag. Every step forward takes time and energy, and it may require the effort of helping others understand. The price of success can be high, but the cost of stagnation is even higher. The lost potential, the heartache and misery, dull relationships, and the discouragement of knowing you are frittering your life away is an extremely high price tag!

❑ Look back at your list of successes. Pick the top three and evaluate the price you paid to pursue them, as well as the price you would have paid if you had not.

Success #1:
What did this cost you?

What would you have lost if you hadn't pursued it?

Success #2:
What did this cost you?

What would you have lost if you hadn't pursued it?

Success #3:
What did this cost you?

What would you have lost if you hadn't pursued it?

❑ Has this exercise sharpened your understanding of your strengths and motivations? If so, in what ways?

❑ Write a summary statement of your past successes and enjoyment.
I see great success when . . .

I am most fulfilled when . . .

Scars from Bad Choices

I remember the story of a little boy who went to visit his grandfather on his farm for the summer. This boy was as mean as a snake! Every time he did something wrong, the grandfather made him hammer a 10-penny nail into the barn door. By the middle of the summer, that door got so heavy it was about to fall off! The grandfather was wise enough to try some new psychology. He told the boy, "Every time you do something good, you get to remove a nail." The new strategy worked. The boy tried his best to do good things so he could take a hammer down to the barn door and remove a nail from that old door. At sunset on the last day of summer vacation, there was only one nail left in the barn door. The boy did one more thing to please his grandfather, so the two of them picked up the claw hammer and headed for the barn door. The boy strained and yanked, and finally he got the nail out. He beamed, "See granddad! The last nail is out. The door is as good as new!"

The grandfather opened the door so the rays of red, setting sunlight came through the door. He gently put his hand on the boy's shoulder and told him, "Son, the nails are gone, but scars remain. You may pull out all the nails, but scars will be left behind." Our choices are the nails, and the consequences we experience are the scars from the bad choices we make in life.

Sometimes I hear people say, "Well, I'll just get forgiveness for doing wrong, and it'll all be over." No, that's not quite the way it works. Certainly God forgives, but there are almost always consequences for our sins. King David knew God had forgiven him for adultery and murder, but he also was convinced, "My sin is ever before me" (Psalm 51:3). I often tell this story about the grandfather and the nails to young people to help them understand that their choices make tremendous differences in their lives. Some of us older folks need to remember that, too.

A scar is not an open wound. It has healed to a great degree. It serves as a reminder of the consequences of bad choices—our own or someone else's. A friend of mine was burned in a fireworks accident when he was just a little boy. His forearm has a large scar. "People notice it and wince when they see it," he commented to me, "but it doesn't hurt anymore. When I see it, I am reminded of a foolish choice I made a long time ago, and I don't intend to make that mistake again!" That's a good lesson from a scar. The amazing thing to me is that God has a way of turning our scars into stars when we give Him our hurts.

Things That Cannot Satisfy

"If only I had a little more money...." How many times have you heard someone say that? In our consumer society, it seems that "a little more money" would solve virtually all our problems. But our headlong pursuit of money and possessions cannot satisfy us. We are always left thirsting for something more. Several decades ago, a meeting of nine of the world's most successful businessmen was held at the Edgewater Beach Hotel in Chicago. In attendance were: Charles Schwab, the president of the largest independent steel company; Samuel Insull, the president of the largest utility company; Howard Hopson, the president of the largest gas company; Arthur Cotton, the greatest wheat speculator; Richard Whitney, the president of the New York Stock Exchange; Albert Fall, a member of the President's cabinet; Jesse Livermore, the most successful stockbroker; the head of the world's largest monopoly; and Leon Fraser, the president of the Bank of International Settlements. This was a power lunch! These men were at the top of the heap. Other men were in awe of their prestige and power. They had it all.

But 25 years later, their lives were in shambles. Schwab lived on borrowed money for a few years before he died in bankruptcy. Insull died a fugitive from justice, penniless in a foreign country. Hopson went insane. Cotton died bankrupt and abroad. Whitney served time in Sing Sing Penitentiary. Fall was pardoned for his role in the Teapot Dome scandal so he could die at home. Livermore and Fraser both committed suicide.

Jesus asked, "What good will it be for a man if he gains the whole world, yet forfeits his soul?" (Matthew 16:26) In other words, if we put the weight of all the world's gold, oil, real estate, and other wealth on one side of a scale, and then we put the value of one person's soul on the other, the scales would tip toward the single soul. Faith, hope, and love—these are the treasures of the soul. And they are worth far more than any amount of money, possessions, prestigious positions, or anything else the world can offer.

This is a lesson we won't learn from commercials, billboards, and magazine ads. We won't learn it from very many of our friends, either. This lesson, however, is one of the most profound we can ever learn. The drive for more and more robs us of the richness of peace and love which our souls crave. A poster in a professor's office states: "Happiness is not having what you want. It's wanting what you have."

Personal and Corporate Purposes

Our lives take on much more meaning and fulfillment when our purposes are aligned with the goals of the company which employs us. I have talked to many men and women who feel like victims of their corporations instead of partners in progress. Many times, the conflict occurs because neither the individual nor the company has a clear, compelling sense of purpose. They simply use each other to

accomplish financial goals instead of being gripped by a passion to make a difference in people's lives. Does that really matter? You bet it does! When both the individual and the company have that outward-focused purpose:
—they have a passion for people.
—motivation levels are high.
—they are creative in problem solving.
—they work as a team because they aren't as threatened by petty squabbling.
—they have the integrity to maintain and protect that purpose.
—success is rewarded and celebrated at all levels.

Even if the corporate culture in which you live lacks that outward focus, you can have a clear, personal purpose statement. Don't let your surroundings squeeze you into its mold! Years ago, I talked to a woman who was an executive in a large company. Her bosses were driving her hard for increased profits. They seemed to care little or nothing about how their attitudes and demands affected employees or customers—as long as profits soared. This woman told me she had several options:

1. To quit and find another job with a company that had a more outward-focused purpose.

2. To sulk, withdraw, and do her job in a minimal fashion.

3. To rally some of her like-minded, victimized fellow employees and form a pity party.

4. To address the problem of purpose directly with her bosses and offer concrete steps for change.

5. To work on her own attitude, sharpen her own sense of purpose, and try to accomplish that purpose through the organization as best she could, with the realization that no organization is perfect.

She said, "To be honest, in my anger and hurt I got together with several others in our company on a regular basis to bash the bosses. That made us feel better—for about five minutes. But I always left those encounters feeling even more bitter and even more victimized. I thought about leaving, but finally, I did some deep soul-searching and decided the problem was more *me* than *them*. I could be a happy, productive, and purpose-driven person even if nobody else in that company supported that perspective. It was the hardest of the options, but that's the one I chose." She continued, "I couldn't do it alone. I asked some close friends to help me by holding me accountable for my attitude and actions. I couldn't have made it without them."

That course of action took a lot of work and a boatload of courage. All of us who are managers will be wise to create an environment that affirms each employee's individual sense of purpose. Our first task may be to help them define their purpose, then we can align that intrinsic motivation with our corporate goals. The results will be greater success, better teamwork, higher productivity, a more positive work environment . . . and most likely, higher profits.

❑ What is your company's *stated* purpose (or mission statement)?

❑ What is its *actual* purpose? How can you tell?

❏ In what ways does your purpose and the company's purpose align? In what ways do they conflict? Explain:

❏ What are your options for dealing with the situation? (How can you avoid being a victim and be more proactive?)

❏ Which option is best for you? Explain:

❏ What resources do you need to help you take positive steps to define and maintain your sense of purpose in your corporate culture?

Overcoming Obstacles

Booker T. Washington said, "I've learned that success is to be measured not so much by the position that one has reached in life as by the obstacles which one has overcome while trying to succeed." Everyone doesn't start from the same point. I have run several times in Atlanta's Peachtree Road Race. When the gun goes off, I'm so far back in the pack that I'm standing near the city limits sign for Greenville, South Carolina! By the time I get to the starting line, the leading runners are about half-way to the finish! Similarly, some of us have had strength and encouragement in our childhoods and backgrounds, but some of us come to that starting point with severe handicaps. We have the idea in America that "all men are created equal." That's a statement we hold dear from the Declaration of Independence, but the reality is that some of us begin on the front row, strong and trim, but some of us are limping even before we get to the starting line. We are already crippled and struggling.

Family relationships can be the launching pad for fulfilling our dreams . . . or they can be the chains that hold us back. Even difficult family relationships, however, can provide springboards for success. Winston Churchill is known as "the greatest man of the 20th century," because his courage and tenacity steeled Great Britain when it was on the verge of being overrun by Nazi Germany. But Churchill's early life was one of the most painful I've ever heard. He was the son of Randolph Churchill, a flaming orator in the House of Commons, and Jennie, a beautiful American woman. Sadly, Winston's parents saw the boy as a nuisance. They were too busy living the exciting, aristocratic British life to be bothered with raising Winston and his brother. They left Winston in the care of a nanny. Throughout his childhood, Winston begged for attention and affection from his parents, but all he received were rebukes and abandonment. He was shipped off to boarding school, where his letters home pleaded for one of them to come for a visit. They seldom did. Young Winston's grades suffered. He developed a severe speech impediment, and he was ridiculed by others boys. He went into the army and found success in the cavalry. Later, after his father died of syphilis and his mother began a series of affairs (including one with the Duke of Windsor, the future king), Winston, too entered politics and became a member of Parliament. Despite his lisp, he became a spellbinding speaker, and he quickly rose in the government to be Chancellor of the Exchequer, only one step away from becoming Prime Minister. His principled views on India's self-rule, however, were at odds with the government, and he forfeited his cherished cabinet position. Churchill then entered his "wilderness years" when he was a political outcast.

During these difficult years, Churchill was almost the only man in all of Britain who foresaw the threat of Hitler's Germany. The government and the British nobility were captivated by Hitler's Teutonic efficiency and inspiring rhetoric. They embraced Hitler as the hope of Europe, even as Churchill's lone prophetic voice foretold of impending war against the German aggression he knew was coming. Churchill's enemies in Britain and in Germany castigated him unmercifully. His circle of admirers was reduced to a pinpoint.

Hitler showed his bloody hand by invading Czechoslovakia and then Poland. Suddenly, Churchill was brought back into government as the Lord of the Admiralty to defend Britain from raw, Nazi power. In only a few months, all of France, Belgium, and Holland were overrun, and British troops cowered at the beach at Dunkirk waiting to be annihilated. In an miraculous operation, almost all the soldiers were ferried across the English Channel by fishing boats, sail boats, ferries, and any other craft the English could get to sea. But they left all their tanks and artillery on the beaches of France. They had saved their lives, but they had precious little to fight with. Now they waited for the invasion which Hitler promised. British morale was gone. Despair pervaded the nation. England was alone, without equipment and facing the greatest army the world had ever known. At the height of the crisis, Churchill was made Prime Minister. His confidence in Britain's future and his gripping rhetoric breathed confidence into his countrymen and turned the tide of history almost by sheer will.

The war raged for five more years until the Allies finally defeated Hitler. If Churchill had not stood strong to unite Britain, the war almost certainly would have been lost. What built such drive into that lion of a man? Certainly his personality was filled with determination and creativity, but his incredible tenacity against all odds was forged in the crucible of rejection. The wounds his parents inflicted on him developed a strength of character that ultimately saved western civilization. That doesn't make parental neglect a good thing. Not at all. But even the darkest moments of our lives can ultimately produce our greatest strengths. Scars can turn into stars. At the end of the war, Churchill was asked to speak at Harrow, the school where he had struggled and failed so miserably as a boy. After a glowing introduction, every eye was fixed on this brilliant, successful leader. He mounted the platform and said, "Never give in. Never give in. Never, never, never, never—in nothing, great or small, large or petty—never give in except to convictions of honor and good sense." And he sat down. That was his message for those school children—because that was the message of his life. Throughout all the failures, abandonment, ridicule, and rejection, Winston Churchill believed it was his destiny to make a difference in people's lives. And he did.

When the prophet Samuel was looking for the next king of Israel, God led him to Jesse's house. Samuel asked Jesse to bring his sons before him. One of them, Eliab, was a tall, strong young man. He looked like a king. Samuel guessed this was the one! But God said, "No. This is not the man. You looked on the outside, but I look at the heart." Samuel was confused. God had led him to Jesse's house to anoint one of his sons as the next king, but none of them would do. Samuel asked, "Jesse, are these all your sons?"

Jesse said, "Well, there's one more—the runt of the family. He's a little freckle-faced, red-headed kid who's tending sheep. His name is David." By his actions, Jesse had said, "These other seven sons of mine are really important. But David? We can do without him."

"Send for David," Samuel told him.

In a while, David came in and stood in front of his frowning father, his glaring brothers, and the smiling Samuel. "This is the one," God told Samuel, "arise and anoint him."

David was rejected by his family. It would be similar to your family having the president over for dinner and you not being invited! David used his time alone with the sheep to develop his relationship with God. And he developed some other skills there, too. He killed a marauding bear and a lion, and these exploits gave him confidence later when he faced another foe—Goliath.

I believe David was deeply hurt by his family, but he didn't let that rejection determine the path of his life. He focused on God's love and purpose for his life, and he became a great king over all his people (including his parents and his brothers!). Some people give us messages that we are stupid, incompetent, and in the way. We are considered the black sheep in the family and compared to other black sheep: "You're going to turn out just like that bum, Uncle Herb!" We may experience the constant, acidic corrosion of these messages, or we may feel the atomic bomb of physical abuse. Or both. On the outside, some people who have experienced these wounds seem to be relatively unaffected, but I believe all of us who experience these kinds of hurts are genuinely and deeply affected. Some of us who have experienced abuse or abandonment limp to the starting line with barely enough strength to stand. Others who have been deeply hurt are determined to never, ever let themselves be hurt again! They are driven to be in control, to be on top, to have power over others . . . and they are often incredibly successful in their efforts. The writer of Hebrews tells us to "lay aside every weight" as we run the race. Take off the "leg weights" of verbal abuse you have experienced, and know that God loves you!

Personality and environment play important roles in how we respond to adverse family relationships. More sensitive people feel the hurts more deeply and are usually more devastated, but they may also be more receptive to the love and nurture they find from caring people later in their lives. Tough people seem to weather the early storms more easily, but they often are so tough that they don't allow themselves to be honest about the pain and get the help they need later in life. Their lives become a series of almost military triumphs and failures, too often devoid of real relationships.

The noted philosopher Soren Kirkegaard said, "We live life going forward, but we understand it looking backward." Looking backward is heartwarming for some, heartbreaking for others. But looking back helps us understand why we feel and act the way we do today. It is a vital piece of the puzzle in discovering our North Star.

When we look back, we can also see how God has directed and protected us, and perhaps how He has used even the darkest moments in our lives to produce strength and sensitivity. We've all heard many times that our lives are like tapestries: We can look at the back and see a mess of dangling strings, but when we look at the front, we can see a wonderful design God is weaving. We need bifocals of faith so we can see, as God sees, the near and the far. Even when we can't make rhyme or reason out of the things in our lives today, we can be sure that God has them sorted out for eternity. Some of our greatest lessons and the deepest wells of character come from the springs of difficulty.

First Memory

Some psychologists tell us that our first conscious memory is very significant and provides a window on our deepest needs and desires. My first memory occurred when I was only about three years old. I was on the porch of our house up in the mountains of North Carolina. Cross-ties were the steps up to the porch from the walkway. I can still see my Daddy bringing me a big orange, iron tricycle. I was so excited! He put it down on the porch for me, then he went inside to clean up. My mother needed to go in and finish fixing supper, but before she closed the door, she turned to me. She looked me square in the eye and said, "Whatever you do, don't ride that tricycle off this porch, Ikey." I nodded, and she went inside. As soon as she disappeared, I backed that big orange tricycle as far as I could. I remember bumping it against the wall. Then I peddled that thing as hard as I could go! I launched it off the porch into thin air! That huge tricycle landed like a ton of bricks! Somehow, I never fell off. It hurt, but I sure couldn't cry. I just kept peddling as hard as I could across the yard. I think this taught me that no matter how hard the fall, you can keep going. (A psychologist may find a different lesson in my experience, but I'm afraid to ask!)

Donald Trump's first memory is of himself and his brother building with blocks. He traded something to his brother for his blocks so he could build his bigger and higher.

Billy Graham's first memory is of his daddy opening his arms and saying to little Billy, "Come to me, son. Come to me." How many times have we seen Billy Graham, with his arms outstretched, say to his audience, "God is a loving Father who says to you, 'Come to Me. Come to Me.'"

(The first time I met Billy Graham, I waited in line for a long time. I was really nervous about meeting such a great man. Then when it was finally my moment to meet him, I introduced myself as "Rike Ikehard." Dr. Graham looked at me and said, "Mmmm. Rike is an unusual name." I said, "It sure is." And I walked away thinking, *What an idiot I am!!!!*)

Family History

In many ways, we are a product of our upbringing. The environment of our childhoods shapes our lives and motivations. It either allows us to blossom or drives us into a mold where we don't fit so well. There are no perfect parents and, in fact, we don't need perfect parents. We need, as author Virginia Satir has said, "good enough parents" who may not give us perfect love, protection, and encouragement, but enough of each to make us feel loved and secure. There are many good books which provide a detailed explanation of the dynamics of family relationships and their profound effects on our lives. We don't have space for that here, but it is instructive to at least touch on this powerful, vitally important topic to show how it impacts our pursuit of our North Star.

Many of us can point to wonderful memories of our childhood homes. We felt loved and safe under our parents' roof, and we can see many strengths in our lives today that are the direct result of those relationships. Others of us have very painful memories of abuse and abandonment, of addictions and rage. The vast majority have checkered memories, full of both good and bad.

A word of caution: I am not advocating a "bash-your-parents" approach. As we become objective about our parents and ourselves, we will be able to assign appropriate responsibility. Perhaps they were at fault in some ways, and perhaps we failed to respond properly at some times. The goals, as always, are honesty, truth, love, and reconciliation. I hope we can focus on the strengths we have gained either by following their example or from learning from their mistakes.

❏ How did your parents relate to each other? How did they show love? How did they show anger? How were problems resolved?

❏ How did your father relate to you? How did he show love to you? How did he discipline you? What effect did your father have on your life?

❏ How did your mother relate to you? How did she show love to you? How did she discipline you? What effect did your mother have on your life?

❏ How did you relate to your siblings? Which ones made you feel strong and loved? Which ones made you feel weak and afraid? Explain:

❏ List each person in your family. How did each one resolve conflict and handle stress?

❏ What would you say was your father's North Star—his dream or his purpose in life—when you were a child? Explain:

❏ What would you say was your mother's North Star—her dream or her purpose in life—when you were a child? Explain:

❏ What strengths are in your life today as a result of your childhood environment? (Which of these were modeled to you? Which did you develop as responses to weaknesses in your home?)

❑ What did your father value above everything else? Explain:

❑ What did your mother value above everything else? Explain:

Birth Order

Many people recognize a pattern in birth order:
- Oldest. Parents have the highest expectations of the oldest child, so this person usually becomes very responsible, effective, and efficient.
- Youngest. The youngest child is the baby of the family and is often pampered and given more freedom and affection than the others. This person often becomes free-spirited, but a bit irresponsible.
- Middle. Middle children feel left out. Expectations of them aren't as high as the oldest child, and they aren't pampered like the youngest. They have to find their own slot in the family and make their own mark in the world. Nothing is sure for them.
- Only. Only children feel like the center of the universe. They get all the attention, as well as all the expectations to be the best and brightest kid in the entire world.

When I speak to an audience, I enjoy asking people to identify themselves according to their birth order. I'll ask, "All you committed, responsible, on-time oldest children raise your hands. All you free-spirited babies of the family—who came to the meeting late—raise your hands. And all the rest of you are middle children in therapy, right?!" One author has observed that the more dysfunctional a family is, the less the birth order pattern applies. For instance, he cites an alcoholic family in which the oldest child is very irresponsible and, in fact, became an alcoholic himself, but the youngest child became the hyper-responsible one in the family.

❏ Where are you in the birth order in your family?

❏ In what ways does the birth order pattern hold true in your family? In what ways is it a bit off? Explain:

❑ Hypothetically, as they grow into adulthood, how would you expect the different children (oldest, youngest, middle, and only) to pursue their North Star? Explain:

Love/Loss History

Our lives contain many high points and low points. It is often helpful to stop and reflect on those times in our lives when we felt particularly loved, and those times when we experienced loss. Keep in mind, there are many different kinds of losses we experience, not just death. We feel the pangs of loss when:

—an engagement is broken off
—a child leaves home
—we move away from friends
—we are fired or don't get promoted as we hoped
—we feel betrayed by a friend
—we experience the ongoing losses of living with an alcoholic parent or spouse
—we experience abuse or neglect
—divorce occurs
—chronic or acute disease strikes
—severe injury impacts our lives

A Love/Loss History gives you the opportunity to chart the significant events in your life and how you responded to them. To the left of the line, list those events or periods of your life in which you felt particularly loved, strong, and secure. To the right of the line, list your losses.

For instance, a man named Jim recorded:

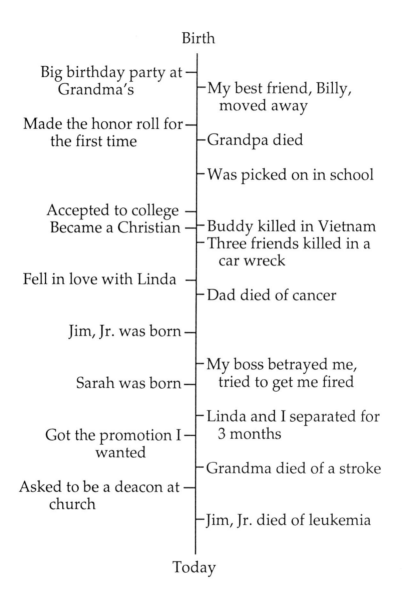

Birth

Big birthday party at
Grandma's

├ My best friend, Billy,
    moved away

Made the honor roll for
the first time

├ Grandpa died

├ Was picked on in school

Accepted to college
Became a Christian

├ Buddy killed in Vietnam
├ Three friends killed in a
    car wreck

Fell in love with Linda

├ Dad died of cancer

Jim, Jr. was born

├ My boss betrayed me,
    tried to get me fired

Sarah was born

├ Linda and I separated for
    3 months

Got the promotion I
wanted

├ Grandma died of a stroke

Asked to be a deacon at
church

├ Jim, Jr. died of leukemia

Today

❑ Take a few minutes to stop, get quiet, pray, and reflect. As you chart your Love/Loss History, you may think of events and people (both positive and negative, pleasant and painful) you haven't thought of in years, and you may think of relatively minor events in your life. If you think of them during this time, it may indicate that they are more important than you previously thought.

Positive   Birth   Negative

Today

❑ Now, list each positive event or loving, supportive person you put on the left side of your chart. For each one, describe how that love or that success made you feel and act at that time.

❑ Are there any patterns in your loves and successes? Explain:

❑ Are there any patterns in how you responded to these loves and successes? Explain:

❏ List each painful person or negative event you put on the right side of your chart, and describe how that loss made you feel and act at that time.

❏ Were there any ongoing losses, such as abuse, neglect, or living with an alcoholic parent or spouse? If so, list and describe these here:

❏ How did these ongoing losses shape your life (motivations, hopes, fears, health, etc.)?

❑ Are there patterns in the types of losses, the intensity of them, or the timing of them? Explain:

❑ Describe the pattern of your responses to these losses.

❑ Which of these losses are "complete," that is, you have grieved them and the "dagger of hurt" has been removed?

❑ Which of the losses still causes you to feel deep pangs of anger or hurt, to cry, or to withdraw?

❑ What have you learned about yourself and your typical grief responses by doing this Love/Loss History?

Summary

Looking back can be an encouraging experience, or it can be painful. Either way, this exercise can be very enlightening. I can look back and see a very checkered past in my family, but through it all, I see many strengths in my life today that are the direct result of my childhood and past adult experiences.

❑ What are the most profound lessons you have learned and strengths you have developed from your past experiences?

4
STAGES AND CHANGES

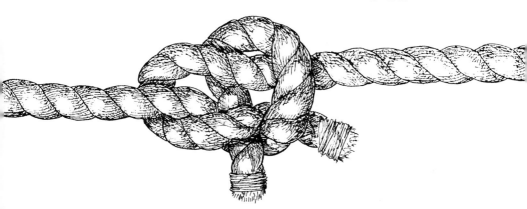

Sociologists identify the different characteristics of each generation: Builders, Boomers, Xers (or Busters), and Millennials. There is no hard line of distinction where one stops and the next one starts, but if you look at the patterns and trends, each generation has its own distinct purpose and style. In the same way, our lives can be divided into stages. They flow from one to another in a seamless fabric of time, but each stage is different and distinct. Psychologist Erik Erikson identified eight stages from infancy to old age. We will focus on the adult stages and show the particular challenges and opportunities of each one.

My life today is much different than it was when I graduated from college. At that time, I was beginning a family and a career. I was just beginning to learn what my strengths were, so my dreams were in a seminal stage of development. Today I can look back on years of experience. My strengths are evident, and so are my weaknesses. I now am able to focus my energies on those things I do well instead of experimenting with activities that may or may not work. In other words, I am much more effective today because I have learned from those earlier stages. My dreams have been forged on the anvil of disappointment, and they have taken flight on the wings of successes and encouragement.

If we understand the stage we are experiencing, we will be more likely to anticipate the challenges and make good decisions. We will understand the dynamics of change for that particular period of our lives. This gives us patience to endure and the drive to keep going when we go through difficulties. Some of us struggle in earlier stages but flourish amid the challenges of later life. Joshua was a man like that.

As a young man, Joshua blended into the crowd. He was a good man, a strong man, but not an outstanding leader. When Moses had the children of Israel poised on the brink of entering the Promised Land, he sent twelve men to do some reconnaissance in the new land. One of them was Joshua. When the twelve men came back to report, ten of them whined, "There are giants in the land, and we're like grasshoppers to them." They had a mental image of themselves being grasshoppers smashed on a windshield, so they said, "Hey, we can't go there!" Did the people of the land of Cana really look at those twelve men and say, "Look at those little guys. They look like grasshoppers!" Probably not, but that's how these ten men saw themselves, and a person's self-perception shapes his attitude, choices, and destiny. In reality, it didn't matter how they appeared to the enemy. Self-perception was the key.

But two of the spies, Joshua and Caleb, were made of stronger stuff. The Bible informs us that they had a "different spirit." They focused on God's ability, not their own shortcomings. These two men said, "That is a wonderful country. Sure, we'll have to fight for it, but God is with us. We can take it!" Faith is our reaction to God's abilities, not our own ability.

As a young adult, Joshua carved out a reputation for hope and strength. Forty years later, Moses died and left the responsibility of leadership of the nation to a man he could trust, a man who had proven he had vision and strength—Joshua. At this time, Joshua realized the promise of his earlier years. His strengths flowered as he led the nation in conquest of the new land. Moses had tried for 40 years to get the people into the land, but Joshua got them there in only a few days.

Joshua went through challenges as a young man. He was not a spectacular leader then, but he was faithful. Later, he was prepared for a key leadership role in his middle adult years, and he rose to meet those challenges. Each of us goes through particular transition periods in our lives in which we face opportunities and challenges. Perceiving those challenges helps us see our choices more clearly and make the best ones we can make.

Let's identify the stages of adulthood.

Young Adulthood (19—30)
Goal: Establishing Intimacy

In this stage, a person focuses on establishing and deepening relationships through courtship, marriage, childrearing, friendships, productive work, and membership in civic and religious groups. The major decisions made during this period, such as mate, mission, and master, shape the direction of the person's life.

To establish this intimacy with a spouse and friends, the young adult needs a wholesome personal identity. This sense of self allows the person to make independent decisions but still be able to maintain and develop the important connections in life. Erikson states the young adult needs to acquire the capacity to commit oneself "to concrete affiliations and partnerships and to develop the ethical strength to abide by such commitments, even though they may call for significant sacrifices and compromises." [1]

If a wholesome identity and the capacity for intimacy are not developed, young adults move:

—*toward people* to gain love and affection (dependence),

—*away from people* to avoid hurt and gain independence or isolation, or

—*against people* to gain power over them (dominance).

All three of these leave the young adult isolated emotionally, and he tends to be egocentric, manipulative, exploitative, and possessive.

Primary Objectives

The primary objectives of young adulthood are:

—developing a strong, positive identity,

—developing strong, affirming friendships,

—having fun,

—enjoying freedom,

—courting and marriage,

—having children,

—embarking on a career,

—determining goals, and

—joining civic and religious groups.

Or they find themselves . . .

—moving toward people out of need,

—moving away from people out of fear, or

—moving against people out of anger.

❏ Circle the primary objectives of young adulthood (above) which you feel you accomplished during that period of your life.

❏ Put a check next to those which you are currently pursuing but have yet to attain.

❑ Can you identify any of the movements (toward, away, and against people) when you were at that stage of your life? Which one(s)? Explain:

❑ Are you currently experiencing any of these movements? Which one(s)?

❑ If so, how is your life affected by these?

Middle Age (30—60)
Goal: To Be Productive

In this very broad age range, the focus is developing carefully crafted ethical and moral principles to enable us to be productive and responsible, to be effective as spouses and parents, and to find fulfilment at work. Middle age adults also desire creative leisure and a deepening spiritual life. In the latter part of this stage, the focus shifts to the desire to pass on what we have learned to younger people.

Psychologist and author Gary Collins makes the following observation about this stage of life: "Research indicates that life changes appreciably between early and middle adulthood. Men, for example, tend to become more reflective and compassionate, less bothered by inner conflicts and external demands, more loving and gentle. Women, in contrast, often become more interested in careers and successful involvement outside the home. In both sexes, according to Erik Erikson, there will be stagnation unless the individual moves to the stage of "generativity"—and active involvement in encouraging and guiding the next generation."[2]

The strong sense of identity and intimacy developed as young adults are essential to fulfilment in the middle adult stage. Without these emotional and relational anchors, middle aged people often become self-absorbed, stagnant, bored, and frustrated, focused on self-gratification and uncaring about others. Self-gratification can take the forms of pursuing multiple sexual partners, alcohol or drugs, unseemly competitiveness at work, strained relationships with spouse and children, the drive to acquire more possessions, and an unquenchable thirst for recognition. All these are evidences of a "mid-life crisis." Disappointments multiply and intensify without relief, and the person, who had so much promise only a few years before, loses focus. Death by inches results if the person doesn't arrest and reverse this trend.

People in the latter parts of midlife are concerned about losing control of their lives—their health, competence, and independence. In her book, *Understanding Men's Passages*, Gail Sheehy identifies the significant—and often devastating—losses men face during these years. She writes, " 'Exit events' begin to pile up in the second half of life—loss of social status, the departure of grown children, sudden deaths of friends. These and other common occurrences are now considered portents of physical problems. The literature remarks on how frequently an individual under high stress—especially a man—is unaware of its existence and its impact on his life."[3]

Middle adulthood can be divided into three distinct parts, each covering approximately a decade of life. In each of these, common issues surface, but each period has slightly different goals to accomplish to stay on track toward fulfillment.

Ages 30—40 Goal: Establish Productivity
—establish values and ethics
—establish long-term goals
—establish career path
—establish a strong relationship with spouse
—establish family lifestyle pattern
—establish community involvement

Ages 40—50 Goal: Evaluate Progress in Productivity
—reexamine values and ethics
—evaluate validity of long-term goals based on real performance
—find meaning in career path, or change careers
—make necessary adjustments in marriage to cope with changes in family life
—relate to teenage children
—find significance in community involvement

Ages 50—60 Goal: The Realities of Productivity
—enjoy or lament ethical choices
—face realities of fulfillment or failure of long-term goals
—face realities of career path
—experience consequences of choices about relationships with spouse and children

—mentor younger generation as they establish their own independence

—find success in community involvement or fade from involvement

❑ Look more at the characteristics of these middle adult stages rather than the somewhat arbitrary age brackets. Are you in a part of middle adulthood right now? Explain:

❑ Circle the challenges of middle adulthood (look at all three parts) which you face today.

❑ Which of these challenges seem most attractive and stimulating to you? Explain:

❑ Which of these seem most threatening to you? Explain:

❏ Are you experiencing any of the evidences of a "midlife crisis" listed in a paragraph above? If so, which one(s)?

Late Adulthood (60+)
Goal: Looking Back Without Regret

In the later years, the focus is on past accomplishments and meaningful relationships. If the person's life has been full of good choices and loving people, this will be a very pleasant and rewarding time. If, however, poor choices and strained relationships clutter the memory, anguish instead of gratitude may fill the older adult's thoughts. If older people see life as a series of failures, broken relationships, missed opportunities, and poor decisions, they may become withdrawn and bitter, waiting sadly for the certainty of death.

When most older people look back on life, they see a checkered pattern. They have choices to make at that point. They can be "half-empty" people and complain about all they have missed, or they can be "half-full" people and give thanks for all the good things. With the reality of approaching death, spiritual life takes on increased importance as the physical body declines.

Common issues of late adulthood are:
—reflecting on life: thankfulness or complaints,
—adequate retirement income,
—declining physical health,
—the death of close friends and family members,
—developing and maintaining rich relationships,
—maintaining creativity,

—maintaining independence,
—making amends to those wronged,
—spirituality, and
—legacy: what am I leaving behind?

❑ Which of these challenges do you face today?

❑ Are you a "half-empty" person or a "half-full" person?
Explain:

❑ What amends do you need to make to resolve past offenses and alleviate guilt?

❑ What is your specific plan for making these amends? (Who, what, when, where, how, and why?)

❏ What are the things you are most thankful for as you look back on your life?

Summary

❏ Go back over all the stages of adulthood. What are the characteristics which best describe your life right now?

❏ Which stage would you say you are in?

❏ What challenges can you anticipate in the next few years for which you need to be prepared?

❑ How will you meet those challenges?

❑ Think over the exercises in the last chapter about past successes, family background, and overcoming obstacles. How has your family background helped or hindered the development of a healthy identity and your ability to form strong, intimate relationships?

❑ Identity and intimacy are the foundations for moving through all of adulthood's stages with grace and dignity. What can you do to develop a more healthy identity (or sense of self)?

❑ What is the right blend of independence and intimacy? How can you learn to have that blend?

❑ What are the highlights of your life up to this point?

5
PERSONALITY AND RISK

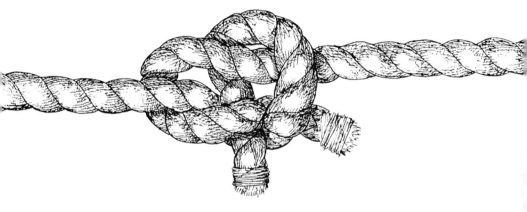

Background, circumstances, and personality all play important roles in shaping our choices. These also determine how we respond to risk and change. I don't mind change. In fact, I create a lot of it! I enjoy it . . . as long as I feel like I'm in control of it, and it's not in control of me. (I have a feeling I'm not alone in that perspective.) If we understand ourselves and the people we are close to at home and at work, we can maximize strengths and minimize weaknesses. We will know what roles are best suited for our particular personalities, and which ones create tremendous stress—and often, failure.

Operating in roles that fit your personality generates enthusiasm and contentment. Of course, no career role perfectly fits a person's personality, but if we find one that closely approximates our motivational style and allows our personality to shine, we will be much more productive and content.

Some of us confuse contentment (being happy with what we have) with complacency (accepting the status quo). A content person can be highly motivated to move forward, to change, to chart new waters in life. A complacent person has lost that drive and creativity. He or she settles for the way things are with a sigh of resignation. Some of us think ambition is an evil, selfish motivation, but ambition is right or wrong based on our objective. If our ambition is to dominate others and get all we can get, then certainly it is misguided. But if our driving ambition is to help people—to give, love and serve—then it is a positive, outwardly focused motivation. It is just as wrong to be complacent as it is to be blindly ambitious. The only difference is that complacent people usually don't hurt others in the overt way that many hard-driving people do.

Take the North Star Personality Profile to get a bead on your particular motivational style. The analysis of your specific profile will show you how you normally respond to risk and how you relate to others. The analysis uses four ships as metaphors for the four personality types: the battleship Missouri, the cruise ship Paradise Star, the sailboat Intrepid, and the research vessel Calypso. Relax and enjoy it. Trust me: You can't flunk a personality profile!

North Star Personality Profile

In each statement, which response BEST describes your actual, typical response?

1. When a task is assigned, I . . .
    __a. take action.
    __b. find the best system to get it done on time.
    __c. find ways to involve others.
    __d. evaluate new ways of getting the job accomplished.

2. In a group of people, I . . .
    __a. enjoy a few deep conversations.
    __b. enjoy being the center of a discussion.
    __c. often become impatient with meaningless chatter.
    __d. often feel uncomfortable.

3. As a member of a team, I . . .
    __a. value order and schedules.
    __b. take charge.
    __c. want everybody to feel good about working together.
    __d. prefer to be delegated a specialized task I can do alone.

4. When I perceive my supervisor or boss is treating me unfairly, I . . .
    __a. become discouraged and pessimistic.
    __b. become harsh and demanding.
    __c. insist on rules being followed, but won't say so.
    __d. try to get others to agree with me.

5. My goal in an organization is . . .
    __a. teamwork.
    __b. getting promotions and raises.
    __c. implementing systems that increase productivity.
    __d. finding creative ways to accomplish goals.

6. When things get tense, I . . .
    __a. find it hard to make decisions.
    __b. don't care what others think and feel.
    __c. talk to those involved to resolve the problem.
    __d. resist any change.

7. When an opportunity arises, I . . .
    __a. enjoy the challenge and am determined to
        capitalize.
    __b. enjoy competition with others.
    __c. need clear goals and procedures.
    __d. need time to evaluate what to do.

8. When a friend is feeling down, I . . .
    __a. ask questions to find out the deeper problem.
    __b. am quick to give advice to fix the problem.
    __c. don't know what to do.
    __d. think my support can help my friend, whatever
        the problem is.

9. I enjoy an environment that . . .
    __a. is flexible and has variety.
    __b. has an organized plan to accomplish goals.
    __c. lets me take action.
    __d. gives me plenty of time to think and plan.

10. My thinking processes can be described as . . .
    __a. logical and ordered.
    __b. varied and imaginative.
    __c. clear and decisive.
    __d. deep and reflective.

11. When I am in a leadership role, I . . .
    __a. like to see lots of activity.
    __b. like to have lots of freedom to do things my way.
    __c. implement a clear system.
    __d. implement a supportive, team spirit.

12. When people criticize me, I . . .
    __a. try to convince them they are wrong.
    __b. blow them off.
    __c. consider if they are right.
    __d. wilt and withdraw.

13. I function best when I . . .
    __a. can concentrate on one task at a time.
    __b. get lots of positive feedback.
    __c. have plenty of time to think through difficult
       decisions.
    __d. can be in charge.

14. In my spare time, I prefer . . .
    __a. to do something active.
    __b. to read a good book.
    __c. to be with friends.
    __d. work on a craft or hobby.

15. I prefer a leader who . . .
    __a. is warm and supportive.
    __b. challenges me to do more.
    __c. provides clear expectations.
    __d. allows me to communicate my opinion and feelings.

16. When a new idea is communicated, I . . .
    __a. want to know how it fits into what I am already doing.
    __b. want to analyze the concept to see if it can be improved.
    __c. want to make it happen.
    __d. am discouraged because I didn't think of it.

17. People would describe me as . . .
    __a. intense and in charge.
    __b. likable and supportive.
    __c. steady as a rock.
    __d. thoughtful and reflective.

18. If I had money to invest, I would . . .
    __a. carefully analyze many options before investing.
    __b. value the input of a professional and do what he says.
    __c. be very conservative.
    __d. be willing to take great risks for the possibility of great rewards.

19. When I am late, I . . .
    __a. feel very guilty for inconveniencing others.
    __b. admit it's a problem, but it doesn't matter much.
    __c. blame others for the problem.
    __d. develop a plan so it doesn't happen again.

20. In a group, when someone asks for my opinion, I . . .
   __a. gladly give it.
   __b. defer to someone else.
   __c. defy anyone to disagree with me.
   __d. carefully consider my answer.

Self-Scoring Chart

Find your responses and circle the ones that correspond with your answers:

	The Missouri	The Paradise Star	The Intrepid	The Calypso
1.	a	c	d	b
2.	c	b	a	d
3.	b	c	d	a
4.	b	d	a	c
5.	d	a	b	c
6.	b	c	a	d
7.	a	b	d	c
8.	b	d	a	c
9.	c	a	d	b
10.	c	b	d	a
11.	a	d	b	c
12.	b	a	c	d
13.	d	b	c	a
14.	a	c	b	d
15.	b	a	d	c
16.	c	d	b	a
17.	a	b	d	c
18.	d	b	a	c
19.	c	b	a	d
20.	c	a	d	b
Totals	____	____	____	____

Evaluation

❑ If any one of the columns contains 12 or more responses, you have a clear personality type. If any two of them together contain 15 or more but neither is over 10 by itself, you have a strong blend of two personality types.

❑ Go back to your answer sheet and examine your responses carefully. Put a check next to 5 or 6 responses that stand out to you as being most indicative of your personality. Based on this profile, write a description of your personality:

Are goals or people more motivating to you? Explain:

Is your communication predominantly direct (forthright) or indirect (you'd rather let your actions do the talking)? Explain:

How do you respond to challenges? (Do they inspire you or threaten you?)

How do you relate to peers?

How do you relate to authority?

How do you relate to those who report to you?

You prefer a work environment that is:

You prefer relationships that are:

Four Personality Types

For millennia, four distinct personality types have been recognized. The ancient Greeks assumed these came from the different body fluids. Later, more sophisticated psychological frameworks were used to identify the blends of task-oriented or people-oriented motivations, and direct or indirect communication styles. For the North Star Personality Profile, we use ships as metaphors of the four behavioral tendencies in people.*

Battleship—The Missouri

In smooth waters, The Missouri is proud, practical, and focused on accomplishing its goals. People who are like The Missouri have a definite mission to accomplish and take action to get the job done. Like a battleship, they are powerful and productive. They assert their authority whenever and wherever it is necessary to make things happen. Command is clear. Decisions usually are not based on subjective feelings, and they are often emphatic and decisive. The guns are ready at a moment's notice to blast anyone who gets in the way.

When battle stations sound, The Missouri goes on full alert! It takes action immediately, often with little reflection, and rarely with the feelings of others in mind. The battleship's mode of operation in crisis is: Ready, fire, aim! It becomes totally focused on getting the job done, not on supporting people in the process of getting this goal accomplished.

---

*The use of the names of these four ships is arbitrary, and in some cases, fictitious. No endorsement or formal connection of any kind is implied by the use of the names of these ships.

Cruise Ship—The Paradise Star

Under normal conditions, The Paradise Star is a party in motion! People who are like the cruise ship are direct in communication and very people-oriented. Relationships, though not always deep ones, are the way of life on board. Everyone wants (and expects) everyone else to participate in every activity. (It looks like a convention of salespeople!) They encourage each other as they engage in good-natured competition for attention. They don't always know exactly where they are, where they are going, or how they are to get there. They just enjoy the ride!

If a storm unexpectedly comes up on the high seas, the passengers run around frantically and talk incessantly! They have forgotten what the captain told them about emergency procedures (they were too busy talking to new friends at the time), so they don't follow the plan for emergencies. Some of them wilt under the pressure and withdraw into their rooms; some convince themselves to "just be positive and it will be OK"; and others become demanding and domineering, but still without a definite plan.

Sailboat—The Intrepid

Nothing is as serene and beautiful as a sailboat cruising on open waters in the sunshine. People who are like The

Intrepid are usually indirect in communication and people-oriented. They, like The Paradise Star, enjoy relationships. The Intrepid has fewer but deeper friendships than the cruise ship. The sailboat is quiet and demur, almost shy, and very responsive to the winds and waves. Detailed charts are studied, and new ones are carefully made for each voyage. The Intrepid is creative and enjoys trying new ways to sail. A deep keel gives balance and stability on the open waters. People who are like these sailboats are loyal friends because of their depth of reflection and commitment to care for individuals.

In a storm, Intrepids are tossed more than other vessels. Their fragile beauty and creativity can be capsized by strong winds and waves, or smashed by other ships. Blown and battered, they may become indecisive, hoping against hope for calmer waters to suddenly appear. The depth of reflection can easily turn to pessimism in the stormy seas.

Research Vessel—The Calypso

For years, Jacques Cousteau's ship, The Calypso, has been recognized as the quintessential research vessel on the ocean. People who are Calypsos tend to be indirect and goal-oriented. They are very analytical and immerse themselves in the details of organization and research. They patiently conduct their experiments until they get the results they need. They insist on following procedures in all circumstances because this gives them focus, stability, and the promise of a useful outcome.

In rough waters, The Calypso implements a carefully constructed contingency plan (which has been rehearsed time after time). It insists on following this plan, no matter what the emergency might be. Flexibility is not even considered as a possibility. Those who fail to follow the designated plan will be silently resented—but seldom confronted so the problem can be resolved.

Risk and Change

Battleships and cruise ships are able to take risks much more easily and more frequently than sailboats and research ships. That's their nature. There is nothing inherently wrong with being a risk-taker or with being cautious. All of us need to learn to take controlled risks. Jesus told a double parable about a foolish builder who took the risk of beginning to build but didn't have enough materials to finish. He also told about a foolish general who went to battle without enough strength to win. (Luke 14:28-33) The Missouri and The Paradise Star both need to think before they take risks, and they need to communicate more clearly with those around them who are more cautious than they are.

The principle of risk is that great risks sometimes—but not always—yield great rewards. Think of Peter in the boat when the disciples saw Jesus walking on the water. Who else among the disciples would take the risk of saying, "Lord, if it's you, tell me to come to you on the water" (Matt 14:28)? But we also know Peter as one who boasted he would never desert Christ, then he denied his Master three times on the night of His arrest. Risk-takers live checkered lives.

Cautious people eliminate many of the losses from foolish risks, but their caution also makes them fail to take advantage of some opportunities. Each of us needs to see what our strengths are in relation to risk and caution, and learn to minimize the downsides of our personality.

❑ On a scale of 0 (Never any risk—Never!) to 10 (Life is an endless series of big risks, hit or miss, sink or swim, wealth or poverty.), rate your comfort level with risks:

     0   1   2   3   4   5   6   7   8   9   10

❑ What are your risk-related strengths? (When and how have you handled risks well?)

❑ What are your risk-related weaknesses? (What are some common problems you have with risks?)

Risk and change are two sides of the same coin. You can't have one without the other. Change is threatening for cautious people, but it is the way of life for others. Here is how each personality type handles change:

The Missouri invites and creates change, but in stormy seas this person may:
—demand to be in control—now!
—demand that people comply.
—make black-and-white, all or nothing decisions.
—refuse to be supportive of others who are struggling with change.
—stay active.
    For smooth sailing, battleships need clear goals, direct communication, and lots of activity.

The Paradise Star also invites lots of change and enjoys it, but when the cruise ship feels out of control, it may:

—demand that people comply.

—argue.

—be defensive.

—become sidetracked.

Cruise ships need support, encouragement, and room to try new things.

The Intrepid avoids change unless it is carefully thought through. When a sailboat feels out of control, it may:

—be unable to make decisions.

—become withdrawn.

—become pessimistic.

—become defensive.

Intrepids need plenty of time to think and prepare, and they require individualized attention to help them cope with change.

The Calypso wants the security of known processes. It feels very uncomfortable with change. When it feels out of control, it may:

—revert back to previous systems to gain security.

—withdraw.

—blame those who institute the change.

—resist change at all costs.

Research ships need structure, few distractions, and clear, measurable expectations.

❑ Which of these vessels most accurately describes you? Explain:

❑ For you to handle change well, you need:

Combinations

Some of us have a clear, distinct personality type, but most of us are a combination of them. For example, every cruise ship needs a captain. The skipper of a cruise ship may be as decisive as a battleship captain, but he wants to command a ship of fun people who genuinely enjoy each other. Or someone on the Calypso may be a bit more creative and reflective than the other highly systematic crewmen. This would be a combination of The Intrepid and The Calypso.

It is also possible that we relate up the ladder of authority at work or other organizations in a much different way than we relate to peers or to those down the ladder. For example, a person may be a gentle, reflective, responsive sailboat with friends but a battleship with employees at work. Or a highly structured Calypso employee may become a relaxed, fun-loving Paradise Star at home.

Relating to Other Ships

Let's take a look at how each ship relates to the others:

The Missouri

• In peacetime, the Missouri enjoys good-natured competition with other battleships. They banter back and forth and challenge each other to do more and better at work, in sports, and anywhere else they can compete. But if the exercises turn to full-scale combat, they hammer each other with the turret guns until one is bludgeoned into submission. One has to win. One has to lose. They fight to the death.

• The Missouri enjoys the light-hearted fun of The Paradise Star as a much-needed R&R from the stresses of command. But if conflict comes, the battleship is quickly annoyed by the cruise ship's meaningless banter and its lack of decisive action.

• In calm seas, the battleship admires the beauty and serenity of The Intrepid, but pity the poor, defenseless sailboat when the mighty Missouri is at war under a head of steam! When the heat is on, the fragile delicacy of the sailboat is only a minor nuisance to the battleship's goals of conquest. The Intrepid is easily capsized by the raw power of the dreadnaught!

• The battleship values the order, information, and effectiveness of The Calypso. In fact, The Missouri often relies on the research ship's calculations and readings to know where to go and how to fight more effectively. But in battle, The Missouri sees the Calypso as far too slow. The battleship becomes impatient and demanding, precisely because it relies so heavily on the Calypso's information and it wants that information NOW!

The Paradise Star

• When the Paradise Star pulls into port next to another cruise ship, it only makes the party that much bigger and more fun! There are more opportunities to encourage people and more opportunities to impress them, too. When two cruise ships collide, however, it is not a pretty sight! They compete for attention, and friendly competition quickly turns nasty.

• The cruise ship is happy to have The Missouri nearby to protect it from any harm and to make necessary decisions, such as where to go and how to get there. But in heavy seas, the dominating character of the battleship greatly offends the gregarious but easily hurt Paradise Star. They resent each other and cast insults at one another.

• The Paradise Star notices the beautiful Intrepid sail by and admires the sight, but then wonders, "Hey, where are all the people?" The cruise ship enjoys relating to the sailboat, but the sailboat just doesn't move fast enough or carry enough people for the cruise ship's taste. In shipwrecks between the two, the cruise ship wonders why the sailboat takes things so seriously and is hurt so deeply.

• The cruise ship is amused by some of the research findings of the Calypso, and if the conversation is kept at a superficial level, they can talk for hours. In reality, they don't have much in common, so when they collide, The Paradise Star blames the Calypso for being careless.

The Intrepid

- Sailboats can have wonderful relationships with other sailboats. They admire each other's rigging and colorful sails. They can talk at length about the intricacies of plotting charts and tricky maneuvers they have seen or made. Both value depth in relationships, but with that possibility comes the risk of deeply offending each other's delicate sensibilities. Fragile feelings are quickly hurt. If the conflict isn't resolved, their delight in rich communication is replaced by deep wounds, anger, and withdrawal.

- The Intrepid admires the raw power of the battleship and enjoys the protection The Missouri affords. But sailboats are, by nature, wary of the dreadnoughts. In any kind of difficulty, rough seas or war, the delicate crafts are easily swamped by the wake or blasted by the guns of the battleship.

- The sailboat might dock near the cruise ship in hopes of engaging in deep, meaningful conversation, but the quiet, reflective Intrepid's hopes are often dashed by the loudness and endless commotion on the luxury liner. The Intrepid is drawn to the conversations on the Paradise Star, but is deeply disappointed these aren't deeper and more meaningful.

- The Intrepid is quiet like the Calypso, and it can appreciate the depth of the research vessel's analysis and research. The sailboat, however, wants more from the interaction than merely swapping facts. The Intrepid wants a deeper relationship, and this expectation either bores or angers the goal-oriented research ship. When the two ships collide, the Calypso turns its analytical guns on the sailboat and blames it for being too sensitive or not getting enough done. The Intrepid feels belittled and betrayed by the harsh criticism.

The Calypso

• The Calypso values the hard work and contributions made by other research ships. Research ships can enhance each other's effectiveness if they will agree to work together amiably. If, however, suspicions arise, the ships become quite competitive. Their highly-tuned analytical capabilities are then used for harsh criticism.

• Research ships function exceptionally well in harbors protected by The Missouri. In this environment, their needs are met so they can provide necessary information to contribute to the battleship's objectives. The high expectations of the battleship, however, can produce torrents of anger if the battleship perceives the Calypso isn't contributing all that is demanded in the time allotted.

• The Calypso is amused by the party atmosphere on board The Paradise Star, but The Calypso often hangs back and doesn't participate in all the festivities. If these ships run afoul of one another, the Calypso resents the empty chatter and meaningless meanderings of the cruise ship.

• The research ship admires the quiet and the precision of The Intrepid. When they talk about plans and details, they have much in common. The Calypso, however, is focused on structure, systems, and meeting deadlines, not creative reflection and meaningful discourse like the Intrepid. Much interaction usually leaves the research ship impatient to accomplish tasks and the sailboat wanting more depth in the relationship.

Sending Signals

One of the most important principles we will ever learn is that effective communication is what is heard, not necessarily what is spoken. Each of the four ships has unique ways of communicating. If they assume other ships communicate in the same ways as themselves, they will often be misunderstood. For instance, the perceptive, reflective sailboat has to "read" the wind and waves. Its life is full of subtleties and nuances. If it assumes that battleships "read" a nuanced message that "I am in your path," it will almost always get run over! On the other hand, The Missouri prefers blunt, direct communication. It may say without a bit of anger, "Get out of my way." The sensitive sailboat would never communicate in this way—even in anger. It makes the assumption that the mighty Missouri is enraged. The sailboat's feelings are hurt, and it withdraws. The Missouri is left wondering, "What's wrong with the sailboat?"

Here are the common ways each ship communicates:

The Missouri prefers the give-and-take of direct, crisp communication. When talking to this person, don't beat around the bush, and don't think too much about this person's feelings. The Missouri would rather hear it straight than have you soft-pedal what needs to be said.

The Paradise Star prefers direct communication, but this person's feelings can be hurt fairly easily. When talking to the cruise ship, take plenty of time to listen (you'll need it!), but don't be manipulated by persuasive words. Stick to your point.

 The Intrepid is an articulate communicator . . . in a safe environment. This person is perceptive and sensitive, and often assumes others are as well.

The Intrepid will shut down quickly if it doesn't feel comfortable. When talking to a sailboat, soften your voice, ask questions, and listen intently.

The Calypso would rather avoid any difficult communication and go back to working the systems. When talking to the research ship, give specifics and be direct. Give time for explanations. There will be plenty!

Opposites Attract, Then . . .

Most marriages and many business relationships are based on the principle that "opposites attract." We are fascinated by someone whose perspective and motivations are so completely foreign to our way of living. Rugged battleships appreciate the delicate motion of a sailboat skimming along with the breeze. The introspective and hard-working Calypso smiles and laughs at the light-hearted fun of The Paradise Star. The fascination pulls us close. Our defenses go down. Sooner or later, the storms rise or the first guns of war sound in the distance, and fascination quickly dissolves into fear, distrust, and anger. Suddenly those differences which were so attractive now seem like tragic flaws!

- We see The Missouri's protective power now as just bullying and strong-arm tactics.
- We see The Paradise Star's enthusiasm and flexibility as shallowness.
- We see The Intrepid's intricacies and depth as weakness.
- We see The Calypso's systematic approach as emotionless rigidity.

Long-term stress has a way of hardening our perception of the worst in our opposite's nature. During those times, we need to remember what attracted us to that person and focus again on the positives. Every personality type has both good and bad, strengths and weaknesses. Perhaps we were blind to the weaknesses at the beginning of the relationship. And more recently, we have been blind to the strengths as wounds and misunderstandings multiplied.

❑ List the significant people in your life—family, friends, and business associates. Identify each person's personality type. What strengths do you appreciate? What weaknesses do you see in that person? What do you need to focus on to improve the relationship?

Person:

Type of ship—

Strengths—

Weaknesses—

I will focus on . . .

Person:

    Type of ship—

    Strengths—

    Weaknesses—

    I will focus on . . .

Person:

    Type of ship—

    Strengths—

    Weaknesses—

    I will focus on . . .

Person:
    Type of ship—

    Strengths—

    Weaknesses—

    I will focus on . . .

Person:
    Type of ship—

    Strengths—

    Weaknesses—

    I will focus on . . .

Use additional paper if necessary.

Background and Personalities

Our family may have been lower middle class by many standards, but we were rich in love and spunk! I never wondered if I was safe, and I never wondered if I was loved. What a gift from my parents! That security has given me the firm foundation to be myself and try new things. Many people, however, have very different stories. On a wide scale from severe abuse to only minor family dysfunction, they have had to learn to cope with unresolved (and often unspoken secrets about) addictions, abandonment, and abuse. The fear, hurt, bitterness, and shame produced in these families shatters (in the worst cases) and erodes (in the less severe ones) that security that each of us needs for our personalities to flourish. For example, a man who had all the signs of a calm, creative sailboat on those rare occasions when he was not stressed lived with the baggage of an alcoholic upbringing. He lived with that internalized tension, and his life exhibited fluctuations between angry control of others and fearful withdrawal from risks. His family background effectively blocked the strengths of his personality.

As I talked about this phenomenon to one man, he commented, "Yeah, I don't even know what my personality really is. I've been trying to prove myself all my life . . . trying to be someone I'm not. I don't know who I am under the thick crust of my anger."

The principle about the relationship between personality and background is this: The more dysfunctional the background, the more clouded the expression of the personality.

❑ How has your background provided a platform for your personality to shine . . . or clouded the expression of your personality?

❑ If your personality has been significantly clouded, who is the real you?

❑ What do you need to do to resolve wounds of the past to allow you to find hope and fulfillment in the present and the future?

On Target (Or Not)

I began this chapter by saying that it is important for our career path to fit our personality type. I want to come back to that now. I know many people who love their careers because it allows them to be themselves and maximize their strengths all day every day. They love their work! I also know people who are square pegs in round holes. One woman I know is a Paradise Star but her job calls for a Calypso. She loves people and enjoys motivating them to take specific steps in their lives. She served for years as a human resources director in a small company, and she was good at it. Somewhere along her career path, someone noticed that she was also good at accounting. In a crisis situation, her employer asked her to handle the books, and she did a masterful job. Her boss slowly took this woman's other responsibilities—the people-oriented jobs she loved—away from her so she could focus on the accounting. For the first year or so, she did well. The new role was enough of a challenge that it stimulated her, and she maintained her network of good friendships. Over the next several years, however, she gradually lost contact with her friends. She still was an excellent accountant, but she grew to despise her work. She told me, "I used to laugh a lot. Not any more. I used to be involved in people's lives. Now I sit at my computer eight to ten hours a day. The job isn't all that stressful, it's just not what I enjoy doing. That's what's stressful!"

We don't need a perfect fit to be happy, but we need a role that fits us well enough to allow us to operate in our strengths a large part of the time. Take a look at your work schedule every day. How well does it match your personality profile?

❏ What percentage of your time at work is spent on:
—taking action, being decisive
—motivating people, selling
—creating, reflecting
—working systems, monitoring

❏ Which of these stimulates you? Which of them saps your strength? Explain:

❏ If you could do any job in the world, what would it be? Explain:

Summary
❏ What have you learned about yourself by doing the North Star Personality Profile?

❏ How will understanding your personality and the personalities of those close to you help you:
—appreciate each other more?

—anticipate difficulties?

—be more understanding?

—make adjustments to communicate more clearly to each person?

❏ What types of people encourage you and help you grow? How do they do that?

❏ What can you do to stop attacking people who are different from you?

❏ What will be some of the benefits of not attacking them?

❏ Complete this statement:
To maximize my personality's strengths, I need . . .

6
THE ROLE OF FAILURE

Failure isn't the problem—it's how we interpret it. There's a world of difference between "I failed" and "I am a failure." One is a statement of fact about an incident. The other is an indictment of identity. Many of us interpret failure as tragedy. It feels so traumatic that we think we will never be the same. We feel a deep, awful sense of shame about ourselves. We determine (again) that we are worthless people who can't do anything right.

For others, failure is not so big a deal. In fact, each failure is just a stepping stone to future success. What's the difference between these two interpretations? I believe it is in the mental "tapes" we listen to. These tapes were recorded in childhood, and we listen to them for the rest of our lives—or until we have the clarity of mind and the courage to replace them.

We all internalize messages we receive from our parents and siblings. These messages might be very positive, such as:
• I love you!
• You are terrific!

- You have great strengths!
- I believe in you!
- Failure is no big deal. Keep going. You'll get where you need to go.

But sometimes the messages might be negative or conditional:

- I can't believe you are so dumb!
- You can't do anything right.
- You don't deserve my time.
- You'd better shape up . . . our else!
- You'd better not mess up again!
- You let me down. I can't depend on you.
- I love you if. . . .

The way to tell what tapes we've internalized is to listen to what goes on in our minds when we've failed. Those who have positive tapes hear things like, "Don't worry about it. You'll do better next time. What can you learn from this experience?" But those who hear negative tapes call themselves all kinds of foul, vile names, and berate themselves for being so stupid and incompetent. Quite a difference!

On a plane one day, I talked to a wealthy, powerful businessman who shook his head and told me, "Why do I drive myself so hard? Why do I kill myself to do one more deal and make one more dollar?"

I asked him, "Did your father ever tell you how much he loved you and how proud he was that you were his son?"

The man burst into tears. He whispered, "I could never please him. I've been living my life trying to earn his love."

The messages we internalize can come from aunts, uncles, and teachers, too. We've all heard the old saying, "Sticks and stones can break my bones, but words will never hurt me." That is a lie! Words hurt deeply. They can crush the soul. I know a man who, when he was a child in school, had a teacher who assigned animals to each child. She told him, "You're a sheep—because sheep are the dumbest animals on earth." This man has never gotten over the hurt of those words. His life has been a continuous string of intense attempts to prove he isn't dumb and incompetent.

Each personality type deals with failure in its own unique way:

- The Missouri accepts failure as a part of the matrix of risk-taking. If, however, the failures are too many or too significant, the battleship goes into attack mode and blasts anything that is perceived as an enemy.
- The Paradise Star is concerned about how other people will view his or her failure. If nobody notices, the cruise ship doesn't care, either. If others call attention to the misdeed, it may vigorously blame others for the failure or scurry to try to get the problem resolved so it will look better.
- The Intrepid tries to avoid failure by careful planning. When failure comes, this person's sensitive nature is deeply shaken.
- The Calypso avoids failure by diligence, preparation, and attention to detail. When failure occurs, this person gets even more structured, perfectionistic, analytical, and critical. The research ship tends to believe the myth: If you plan properly, it will always work out.

Reactions and Responses

If we interpret failure as a colossal statement about our identity, we will react (or overreact) to it in any of several ways, including:

- Denial: "What failure? It didn't happen."
- Minimizing: "Oh, that's no big deal. Who cares?" (But we are dying inside with guilt and shame.)

- Making excuses: "Hey, I couldn't help it. Give me a break."
- Blaming others: "It wouldn't have happened if Sarah hadn't messed up. It's *her* fault."
- Withdrawing: In acute embarrassment, we avoid interaction with those who know or who might bring up our failures. Sometimes we leave the room, but sometimes we avoid them by reading newspapers or watching television. We may be in the same room, but we avoid any meaningful or threatening conversation.
- Driven: Instead of wilting and withdrawing when we fail, some of us are driven to prove ourselves. We become obsessed with making sure the label *failure* doesn't stick to us, and we bulldoze anyone and everyone in our path. The intensity level is matched by the activity level. We work like crazy to be sure we don't fail again.
- Pervasive anxiety: Those who live with the internalized messages of not being loved and not feeling competent almost always experience free-floating anxiety and anger. The original causes of the fear, hurt, and anger may be long forgotten, but offense has piled on offense, and the person lives in a quagmire of tension.
- Learned helplessness: Some of us have internalized the message, "You're incompetent! You can't do anything!" And we've quit trying. We've learned to be helpless, letting other people make our decisions for us. Avoiding responsibility, however, doesn't make us pleasant and thankful. We resent people telling us what to do at the same time we demand that they make our decisions. We drive them and ourselves crazy!
- Hurt people hurt people: This principle of relationships is all too common in many family and business relationships. Those who are victims of failed relationships become the victimizers of others. Most typically, we who have been

hurt in difficult childhoods then communicate conditional love to our own children. We may despise how we were treated, but we copy that same (or perhaps a different but equally hurtful) behavior in how we treat our own spouse and children.

• Spiritualizing: Conscientious Christians often use passages like Romans 8:28 to say, "See, God will make it work out just fine." But that's not what this passage is saying. It means that God will use the tragedy or failure to teach us a meaningful lesson . . . if we will pay attention with a tender heart and let Him speak to us.

These ways of reacting to failure may have been modeled to us in childhood, or perhaps these are the expressions of the darker sides of our personalities. We can learn to respond to failures more constructively. Here are some things to remember:

Accept Responsibility

Don't deny, and don't blame others for your mistakes. Learn to say those three little words: "I was wrong." If we insist on avoiding responsibility, we won't learn any valuable lessons from the failure, we will prolong the pattern of lying to ourselves, and we set a bad example for those around us. Those are powerful motivations for being honest! This doesn't mean we accept responsibility for other people's failures. We need to be objective and assign appropriate responsibility to each person involved. Then we can choose to deal with our own responsibility appropriately. Philosopher, humanitarian, and physician Albert Schweitzer said, "A man can do only what he can do. But if he does that each day, he can sleep at night and do it again the next day."

Look to God

God's love never fails, and He is a forgiving God. We can learn wonderful lessons if we put ourselves in His gracious hands. Think of the Prodigal Son (Luke 15) who failed his father miserably, yet his dad (as a picture of God) embraced him and welcomed him back home. In that loving environment, we are free to listen to wise instruction from our Heavenly Father.

Sometimes God allows failure to cause us to trust Him instead of our own abilities. In those times, He often asks us to get up and try something that truly scares us! We don't see how it can work. We have such few resources. We don't have a clear plan, but when God tells us to step out on nothing. He'll either provide something to stand on, or He'll teach us how to fly!

God may have a special message for us in our failure. He may use it to prune our selfishness and make our motivations more pure. Theologian A.W. Tozer wrote, "God may allow His servant to succeed when He has disciplined him to a point where he does not need to succeed to be happy. The man who is elated by success and is cast down by failure is still a carnal man. At best his fruit will have a worm in it." In our failure, we are wise to say, "Lord, I'm listening. I'm open to learn whatever it is You want to teach me." If we fail to learn this time, God will keep us in school until we pay attention.

God is vitally interested in shaping our view of success. Former Secretary General of the United Nations Charles Malik said, "Success is neither fame, wealth, nor power; rather it is seeking, knowing, loving and obeying God. If you seek, you will know; if you know, you will love; if you love, you will obey."

Replace Your Tapes

When those old tapes start turning in your mind, stop the machine! Grab those thoughts and toss them out. But remember, nature (and our thought life) abhors a vacuum, so replace the tapes with new ones. Memorize quotes about moving forward, about God's love and purpose in your life, and anything else encouraging to you. This is where the war must be won—in your thought life. Fight hard!

Learn Your Lessons

Failure is an unwelcome guest, but it can be our greatest teacher. When we stop denying, minimizing, blaming, and all the other reactions which are harmful to us and others, failure can teach us some of the greatest lessons of our lives. We may learn to approach risks differently. We may learn to deal with certain people differently. We may learn to maximize our strengths more effectively. And we just may learn that failure is not the end of the world!

For the apostle Paul, difficulties were a necessary part of learning and growing. He learned to see them as an essential aspect of character development. He wrote to the Romans, ". . . we also rejoice in our sufferings, because suffering produces perseverance; perseverance, character; and character, hope. And hope does not disappoint us, because God has poured out His love into our hearts by the Holy Spirit, whom He has given us" (Romans 5:3-5).

How do you and I respond to failure and suffering? The apostle Paul rejoiced because he anticipated that he would grow deeper and stronger as a result. We, too, can have that same perspective.

Try Again

If we have a proper view of failure, we won't be devastated by it. We will get up, dust ourselves off, learn from the situation, and try again. Every play in a football game doesn't go for a touchdown, and even Michael Jordan hits less than half his shots from the field. A baseball player is considered great if he gets a hit three out of ten trips to the plate. Maybe that's a good rule of thumb for some of us, too. Keep trying, and keep trusting God to give you wisdom and direction.

We all remember Abraham Lincoln as one of the (if not *the*) greatest presidents in our nation's history. His tenacity and drive brought the Union through the Civil War. At several points, the war seemed lost to the South's superior field leadership, but Lincoln struggled to keep his administration focused on the ultimate goal of winning the war. Many of us know a little of his presidency, but few of us are familiar with the fact that winning the presidency was one of very few successes he had in his life. History records that his experience was one failure after another:

—in 1831, he failed in business,

—in 1832, he was defeated in a race for the Illinois state legislature,

—in 1833, he failed in business again,

—in 1835, his sweetheart died,

—in 1836, he had a mental breakdown,

—in 1838, he was defeated in a race for speaker of the state legislature,

—in 1840, he was defeated in a race for elector,

—in 1843, he was defeated in a race for the United States Congress,

—in 1855, he was defeated in a race for the United States Senate,

—in 1856, he was defeated in a race for the United States vice presidency,

—in 1858, he was defeated by Douglas for a United States Senate seat,

—but in 1860, he was elected president.[1]

During his presidency, Lincoln faced an organized uprising among members of his cabinet, his wife Mary had a mental disorder, and his beloved son Tad died from a disease. In the war, Lincoln's generals proved singularly inept and lost battle after battle to the ill-equipped but well-led Southern forces. Through it all, Lincoln believed he was a man of destiny. His purpose never swerved, and he is known today as a great hero of our history.

Ruin, Recovery, and Rebound

Failure brings ruin if we don't get up and try again, but we can also experience tragedy if our misguided pursuit of success causes us to lose what is most precious to us. An African farmer named Ali Hafed wanted to find fame and fortune in diamonds. He sold his farm to buy equipment and provisions for his search. He was so consumed with his search that he neglected his family, and they left him. For years, Hafed searched all over to find diamonds, but he found precious few. His money ran out. He was penniless and destitute, without his family and without hope. In despair, he drowned himself in the ocean. One day a man walked across the Hafed family farm and saw an unusual stone. He showed it to a merchant who told him it was a diamond! The man looked further and found another diamond, and another, and another! There were literally acres of diamonds on Hafed's farm. Hafed had read geological charts and talked to countless people to find the right places to look for diamonds, not realizing that his own farm had the characteristics to produce good diamonds. But Hafed never bothered to look on his own property. He thought riches must be found somewhere else, and in the process, he lost true riches: his family and his self-respect.[2]

We can recover from failure if we have the tenacity to keep believing and try again. Sometimes, the odds seem very long, but as a friend of mine said, "Funny things happen to those people who refuse to quit."

Eddie Rickenbacker, a World War I ace and the most famous American pilot of his day, is a great example of someone who refused to quit. Years after the war, he and a group of others were flying across the ocean, and their plane crashed. For days the survivors drifted in a raft with no food or water. Rickenbacker tried to encourage them to stay strong and trust God. One day they were praying for food, and a seagull landed on Rickenbacker's head. He reached up and grabbed the bird. They ate the flesh and used the entrails to catch fish so they would have more food. And they lived. During the ordeal, they were faced with death day after day. Many of them wanted to give up, but Eddie Rickenbacker refused to quit. He kept looking for God to provide opportunities to meet their needs.

In some situations, we can rebound and turn a negative into a glorious positive. This, I believe, is the real message of failure. No matter how bleak the night, a new day is coming full of promise and the certainty of the grace of God. Harland Sanders was looking forward to a comfortable retirement. He had worked hard all his life. It was now time to go fishing. He opened the envelope of his first Social Security check and stared at the amount. *Is that all?* he wondered. *I can't live on this!* He had to do something. Sanders got his mother's recipe for fried chicken and started selling it around the neighborhood. Soon he opened a restaurant, then another and another . . . and as they say, the rest is history. The Colonel looked despair in the face and refused to give in to it.

Failure can produce a firm conviction to help people. Famous preacher D.L. Moody spoke in his Chicago church on the topic, "What will you do with Christ?" At the close, he asked them to think about it for the next week. That night, Mrs. O'Leary's cow kicked over the lamp and hundreds of people, including some from Moody's church, died in The Great Chicago Fire. Moody was shaken by the experience. He said, "Someday, people will rise up in judgment against me because I made them think they had another week to live. But they didn't." From that day on, Moody became a passionate preacher for people to decide then and there for Christ.

Victor Frankl is a prime example of someone who let tragedy shape his life in a powerfully productive way. Frankl and his family were captured by the Nazis and sent to concentration camps during World War II. All but one member of Frankl's family—his sister—died in the ovens or work crews of those camps. Day after day, Frankl watched people respond to the horror, filth, fear, and impending death. Frankl said, "When I stood naked before the guards, feeling ridiculous, I thought, *They cannot make me hate them. As long as I can choose my attitude, they don't control me.*" Even though hundreds and thousands were dying around him every day, Frankl focused on what he would do when he got out of the prison camp. He determined he would travel and deliver a series of lectures on his survival of the camp. Frankl noticed that those who lost hope died most quickly from exposure and overwork. Those who clung to hope of the future had the best chance to live, unless, of course, they were sent to the ovens. One man set a date in his mind that he was convinced they would be liberated. He eagerly anticipated that day, but when it came and passed, the man was devastated and died the next day. Frankl developed the perspective that he refused to allow the Nazis to take away his dignity and humanity, his right to choose. He said, "The last human freedom is our ability to choose our attitude in any set of circumstances." Even in the midst of unspeakable oppression, irrational carnage, and desperate hatred, Frankl refused to allow these things to steal away his fundamental ability to choose to hope. After his release from the concentration camp, Frankl became a psychiatrist in his native Austria. He was Professor of Neurology and Psychiatry at the University of Vienna Medical School. Victor Frankl wrote over 20 books, including *Man's Search for Meaning*.

Helping Others Learn From Failure

One of the greatest gifts we can give our spouses, children, and friends is wisdom about failure. When they mess up—and especially when their mistakes affect us directly—we can be a breath of fresh air and create a classroom of learning by responding properly to them.

Don't overreact. Keep your voice and your emotions under control. Ask questions and listen intently, but be sure the questions are not accusatory. The best ones to ask are positive, such as, "I know you didn't intend to hurt anyone. Would you explain what you were thinking?" or "What lessons have you learned from this?"

Don't bring up the failure again and again to shame the person as a motivation. It may motivate, but the end result will be to drive the person away from you. Help others determine what their goals are, then help them take specific steps toward those goals. End any conversation about failure with plenty of affirmation and a hug to show your unconditional love. You may not have received these encouragements from others, but there's nothing keeping you from giving them to others who need them.

❑ What are the messages you heard and internalized as a child?

❑ Based on your personality, how do you typically interpret failure? (What does it mean to you?) Explain:

❑ How do you usually respond to failure? On a scale of 0 (never) to 10 (all day every day), rate your responses to failure.
I usually respond to failure by:
Denying it
    0 1 2 3 4 5 6 7 8 9 10
Minimizing it
    0 1 2 3 4 5 6 7 8 9 10
Making excuses
    0 1 2 3 4 5 6 7 8 9 10
Blaming others
    0 1 2 3 4 5 6 7 8 9 10
Withdrawing from others
    0 1 2 3 4 5 6 7 8 9 10
Being driven to succeed at all costs
    0 1 2 3 4 5 6 7 8 9 10
Experiencing pervasive anxiety
    0 1 2 3 4 5 6 7 8 9 10

Avoiding responsibility through helplessness
    0   1   2   3   4   5   6   7   8   9   10

Hurting people who hurt me
    0   1   2   3   4   5   6   7   8   9   10

Spiritualizing
    0   1   2   3   4   5   6   7   8   9   10

❑ Is it hard for you to accept responsibility for your failures? Explain:

❑ When you fail, do you instinctively turn to God or turn away from Him? Explain:

❑ When the old tapes begin to play after you've failed, what names do you call yourself? (You might want to write in code here!)

❏ Do you think these names you call yourself when you fail are an indication of your real sense of identity? Why or why not?

❏ What are some new tapes you can memorize and plug in when the old tapes are playing in your mind?

❏ List six significant instances when you have failed.
#1 Event:
What factors led to your failure?

How did you interpret the event?

How did you respond?

What lesson(s) did you learn from the experience?

#2 Event:
What factors led to your failure?

How did you interpret the event?

How did you respond?

What lesson(s) did you learn from the experience?

#3 Event:
What factors led to your failure?

How did you interpret the event?

How did you respond?

What lesson(s) did you learn from the experience?

#4 Event:

What factors led to your failure?

How did you interpret the event?

How did you respond?

What lesson(s) did you learn from the experience?

#5 Event:
What factors led to your failure?

How did you interpret the event?

How did you respond?

What lesson(s) did you learn from the experience?

#6 Event:
What factors led to your failure?

How did you interpret the event?

How did you respond?

What lesson(s) did you learn from the experience?

❏ What (if any) are the common factors in these six events? (common types of failures, causes, responses, lessons, etc.)

❏ What are the greatest lessons you have learned from failure?

❏ What are the lessons you still need to learn?

❏ Who can help you learn these important lessons?

7

NORTH STAR PRINCIPLES

Change is inevitable. Whenever possible, we need to anticipate it and respond to it properly so *we* can control the outcome instead of *it* controlling us. And when we can't control the outcome, we need insight and courage to let that change become a part of the beauty of the fabric of our lives. I want to elaborate on the North Star Principles as a template for how we can effectively handle change.

Embrace Risk as a Way of Life

Battleships and cruise ships embrace risk . . . maybe too much! And sailboats and research ships avoid risk like the plague. The risk-prone may feel completely comfortable with a rush of adrenalin as they wait to see if their gamble has paid off, but they often are unaware of how their ventures affect the people around them. When they fail (and make no mistake, risk-takers fail often), they get blasted by the cautious ones. And if they are blasted often enough, they may lose their sense of adventure and their willingness to try new, creative ventures. Withdrawal may seem just fine to the cautious ones, but battleships and cruise ships aren't meant to function while tied to a dock or anchored in the harbor. They are meant to steam off . . . to war or for fun! If they feel shackled, they get sullen, angry, and discouraged. Battleships and cruise ships need to do two things to enjoy their risk-taking: (1) Be a bit more cautious and take controlled risks; and (2) Make sure others are informed. That will eliminate a lot of the problems.

Sailboats and research ships also need to embrace risk as a way of life, but they come at it from the opposite directions. They ask plenty of questions to make sure everything is right, but even then, they are reluctant to step out. The concept of controlled risks is important for them, too. The control factor limits the risk to reasonable levels, but at some point, they need to overcome "analysis paralysis" and take action. Their risks usually are fairly safe, and they work out a much higher percentage of time because these people have done a lot of homework before the decision has been made.

Goals involve risk. If you try to avoid all risk, you'll never attempt anything at all. You become numb and dull. You lose love, fun, excitement, and fulfillment.

Love involves risk. There's only been one perfect person, so there is risk in being a friend to anyone. We will all be disappointed from time to time in relationships. Sometimes the other person misrepresents himself, and sometimes we simply want more than the other person wants to give. We need to avoid "black-and-white" thinking that assumes a person is all good or all bad. When we believe this, we tend to be either all *in* or all *out* of a relationship. A sure sign of maturity and wisdom is the realization that we are all shades of gray. My mother used to say, "There's so much bad in the best of us and so much good in worst of us that it hardly behooves any of us to talk about the rest of us." One of the things I tell my daughters is: Be slow in choosing your friends, and even slower in leaving them.

There is no formula to eliminate all risks in life. Race car driver Mario Andretti has said, "If you ever have it all under control, you aren't really racing." If we have everything in life under control, we aren't really living.

Take Responsibility

We usually think of taking responsibility for the outcome of our efforts, but preparation is equally important. Legendary football coach Vince Lombardi said, "The will to prepare to win is more important than the will to win." Preparation is hard and often lonely work. We all want to win, but we need to take responsibility to do whatever it takes to put ourselves in a position to take advantage of our opportunities . . . instead of blaming everyone else for letting us down.

Don't blame your DNA, your parents, your children, or your boss. You may have experienced a tragic childhood. Your spouse may be an adulterer or a bum (or both). Your children may have rejected you. You may have experienced terrible abuse and abandonment, and your heart may be broken. You may have let other people make all your decisions for you, and now you are angry at them for not making good ones. Unresolved hurt and anger leave you a victim with a big hole in your heart. To fill this hole, victims demand three things: justice, compensation, and guarantees.

• Victims demand that their offenders be punished. The sentiment is, "It's just not fair for me to suffer and the offender to get off scott free!" The victim won't be satisfied until that person feels plenty of hurt for what he or she has done . . . but no matter how much pain that person feels, it never seems to be enough for the victim's sense of justice.

• Victims demand that other people fill up the holes in their hearts. They go from relationship to relationship, from job to job, expecting people to give them the love and security they have always wanted. But these other people didn't sign up for that! And besides, they had no idea it was expected of them. When they fail to fulfill that role, the victim sees it as just another wound by an uncaring person.

• Victims demand guarantees that they will never be hurt again. They enter relationships with lofty expectations, and of course, no one can meet their desires. So again, the demands go unfulfilled and more expectations are shattered.

By making these unspoken demands on others, victims sabotage virtually every relationship in their lives. Hurt follows hurt, and the demands become even more intense. Each subsequent relationship is subject to a self-fulfilling prophesy beginning with lofty hopes and ending with shattered dreams.

You may be a victim, but you don't have to stay a victim. Find a counselor or support group that will help you resolve the wounds of your past. Then you can rise above the hurt and pain. You can learn to listen to new messages and carve out a new life. No one said this process is easy. It requires more courage than almost any other journey I know, but it's worth it!

We are captains of our own ships. If we are content to take responsibility for our own choices, we can enjoy the victories and learn from the defeats. We will be thankful for the good times and the good friends we find along the way. We'll look at the brighter side of life and learn to laugh. We can direct our own destinies and stop taking ourselves so seriously.

All of us need encouragement and wisdom from trusted friends as we try to sort out our responsibilities and try to find balance in life. You may know people who will serve that role for you. If not, pray and ask God to lead you to mature, godly people who "have been around the block" a couple of times. Their insights will help you sort out the many questions you may have about these issues.

If we want God to bless us with something great, we have to prove ourselves by being trustworthy in the small things. Great doors of opportunity swing on tiny hinges of obedience. How much integrity do we have when nobody is looking? Are we willing to shave numbers off tax returns and expense reports if we think we can get away with it? And we may get away with it . . . for a while. We may even get away with it for our whole lifetimes, but there will come a day when each of us will give an account of our lives to God. On that day, the secrets will be revealed. The choices we make in our closets today will be proclaimed on the housetops on that future day. I sure want that to be a happy day, don't you?

Be Honest About Your Emotions

Paradise Stars and Intrepids are usually more aware of their emotions than the more goal-oriented Missouris and Calypsos. Quiet, reflective sailboats are guarded in their interactions, but cruise ships don't mind telling the world how they feel! The vast majority of us, even the Paradise Stars, tend to wear masks to hide how we really feel about people and situations. In fact, we have worn those masks so long that they have become permanent fixtures. We don't have a clue what's underneath them. Monica Lewinsky, the young intern who boasted of sexual indiscretion with President Clinton, said about her family, "We've always lived a lie."

In the Roman theater, the cast of actors was all male. To play the role of women, or perhaps to play the role of anyone who looked quite different from themselves, they put on a mask. This was called "playing a hypocrite." The word *hypocrite* used to mean only that a person wore a temporary mask to play a part in a play. It has come to mean "phony" or "pretending to be better than we are."

We experience tremendous stress in trying to be somebody we're not. It is like trying to hold balloons under water. We may be able to wrestle one or two beneath the surface, but sooner or later, one pops up . . . usually with intensity! In the same way, eventually our mask of the calm, competent person falls off, and the hurt and angry actual face is seen . . . but only for a moment before the mask is quickly put back on. Here are some masks people wear:

- We wear the mask of a hero, but we are afraid to fail.
- We wear the mask of a comedian to hide our hurt and to divert attention from harsh realities.
- We wear the mask of someone completely in control, because we are terrified of being out of control.
- We wear the mask of a nice, accommodating person, because we want to avoid conflict at all costs.
- We wear the mask of a person who never fails, because we only feel safe if everything goes perfectly.
- We wear the mask of a caring person, because we hope that will win appreciation from those we help.
- We wear the mask of an incompetent slob, because nobody expects much from somebody like that.
- We wear the mask of a rebel, because it makes people admire us from a distance.
- We wear the mask of rage, because we want people to be controlled by our anger.
- We wear the mask of a shy, withdrawn person, because most people won't hurt somebody who is so fragile.

The stress of trying to be somebody we're not is a never-ending battle. We struggle to keep our secrets and put on that good face day after day. Some of us fight this battle our whole lives, but some of us are worn down by the struggle. Physicians tell us that the vast majority of medical illnesses have psychological and emotional components. Many of the stomach problems and headaches we experience are the direct result of our bodies reacting to stress. And the struggle to wear our masks lowers our resistance to all kinds of other diseases. The relational losses are just as significant. When we insist on wearing masks with friends and family, we cannot develop genuine trust and intimacy. The laughter and safety we so desperately desire is out of arm's reach . . . until we take off our masks and risk being real.

Honesty allows us to face our fears and live in emotional integrity. We may realize a depth of hurt and anger we never knew was there (or maybe we did!), but as those hurts are healed, we also can experience more love, joy, and contentment than we thought possible. How do we start? Some of us simply need to share our feelings with a trusted friend. Others need to start by identifying a feeling or two! What emotions have you felt as you read these pages about feelings?

We tend to make one of two opposite mistakes regarding our emotions: We either repress them and act like they don't exist, or we are controlled by them. Emotions are signals of what is going on in our hearts. We need to pay attention to them, but we don't have to let them dictate our decisions and relationships.

Consider using the list of feelings on the next page to help you keep a "feelings journal" to chronicle your emotions each day. If you tend to repress your feelings, these words will help you put labels on what you feel. If you are controlled by your emotions, you will gain insights that will help you break unhealthy patterns of responses.

Feelings Word List

Loved	Ashamed	Frustrated
Afraid	Frightened	Brave
Warm	Happy	Awful
Worried	Shy	Curious
Caring	Excited	Sensitive
Patient	Understood	Terrible
Confused	Pleased	Mad
Scared	Guilty	Daring
Important	Mean	Wonderful
Violent	Comfortable	Gloomy
Angry	Loving	Encouraged
Special	Upset	Hateful
Hurt	Sympathetic	Uncomfortable
Strong	Discouraged	Different
Embarrassed	Moody	Bad
Jealous	Silly	Enraged
Understanding	Nice	Relieved
Thankful	Relaxed	Hopeless
Worthless	Suspicious	Bitter
Secure	Delighted	Alone
Weak	Optimistic	Trapped
Bored	Helpless	Worthy

I know what you're thinking. The ones who don't need this list are thinking, *This is great! Somebody understands how important my feelings are!* And the ones who desperately need to be honest about their emotions are thinking, *What a waste of time! Let's move on to something important.* God has made us in a wonderfully complex way, and we can become the people He designed us to be only if we give adequate attention to each aspect of our lives. Emotions are an important part of that complexity. The positive and pleasant ones usually indicate that we are moving forward on the right track. The negative and painful ones are like red lights flashing on the control panel of our cars. They mean: "Pay attention! Something is wrong here! You need to have your life serviced!" Value your feelings, but don't live by them. They are a wonderful, God-given gift to provide zest to life and indications of trouble. Pay attention!

Former Israeli Prime Minister Golda Meir recognized the importance of being honest about our emotions. She said, "Those who do not know how to weep with their whole heart don't know how to laugh either."

Never Stop Learning

We may have graduated from high school, college, or graduate school many years ago, but we can be life-long students. I can tell when I'm with somebody who is really alive. The person has read a new book and wants to tell me about it. He has found a new hobby and is excited about developing new skills. She is gaining fresh insights on her career by attending a seminar. He is taking classes at a nearby college just to keep sharp in an area of interest. My friend, noted speaker and writer Ira Blumenthal, told me, "Real power is in the hands of the learning, not the learned." When learning is past tense, we are dying intellectually. But the vigorous pursuit of knowledge and new skills gives us a fresh infusion of energy and enthusiasm.

I've noticed that people who have a driving sense of purpose in their lives are good learners. They are highly motivated to read and study. They are sponges, asking questions and trying new techniques. One friend of mine jots down notes all the time about sailing. Years ago when he was first absorbed with his passion, he came home from trips with his pockets bulging with scraps of paper full of notes about rigging, sails, types of boats, and exotic destinations. After a while, he became more systematic in his approach. He began keeping notebooks and then developed a filing system so he could keep track of his knowledge. Today, if you want to know anything about sailing, you can ask this guy. He probably knows!

Our interests are as varied as we are, and each of us can have several compelling subjects or skills we want to explore. I love to read history. The intricate lives and motivations of great people have always fascinated me. That's why I weave stories about people into almost every talk I give and every book I write. Hobbies, sports, travel, finance, health, gardening, and the whole world of other interests are there for the taking. What wonderful complexity God has given us, and what incredible opportunities we have to explore and experience them!

The focus of some people is crystallized in times of crisis. When they, or one of their family members, is diagnosed with cancer, they devour books and research articles about the disease and the cure. A crisis sharpens the mind and invigorates the heart to learn so we can help those who are hurting.

Some of us have cut off ourselves from stimulation and challenge, and we have become emotionally and intellectually stunted. Bonsai trees are aberrations of nature. They grow, but they never become what they were meant to be. Bonsai gardeners cut the roots and shape the plant so it is stunted and small. It is cute and interesting, but to me, there's something odd about an 18 inch maple tree that would have been 50 feet tall in the wild. Similarly, the lives of some of us are equally stunted. We move through our lives in an emotional fog. We do our work, then come home and crash on the sofa and watch television. We go to a movie or two and attend church or some other civic event from time to time, but we are spectators in life, not participants ... watchers, not players. I've heard the excuses that people are tired and they need a break. I've used those excuses myself! But my life is so much richer when my purpose drives my mind. When I have an objective (like writing this book), it is amazing how much more aware I am of news stories, articles, and things people say. Sometimes, of course, we need to take a break, relax, and veg-out, but if vegging out is a way of life, we are missing out on a huge chunk of the abundant life.

The remedy is not just to decide to read, learn, and grow. The pursuit will be a short one if there is no heart for it. The main remedy is to find or refine our purpose in life so passion is kindled in our hearts. That's what gives us the enthusiasm to turn off the television and dive into projects that enrich our hearts, minds, and souls. If we don't read, grow, and think for ourselves, we become echoes, not voices.

Value Meaningful Relationships

Love makes the world go round. I believe that, but then, I'm a Paradise Star! Goals and relationships must go hand in hand, and they must be balanced if we are to have meaningful lives. Most of us naturally gravitate toward one side or the other, but we need to reach out to the other side. God has made us relational beings to love, give, and serve one another. History is filled with stories of people who accomplished great goals but who counted their lives as empty if they didn't find true love along the way. I talked to a CEO not long ago who told me about the ups and downs of his company. "A couple of years ago," he observed, "our company did extremely well. We made a lot of money, and we gave nice bonuses to our employees. But during that time, our employees were at odds with each other, and the mood at our office was tense and discouraged. Over time, some of our employees were replaced. Recently, we had a significant setback for the company, but the employees held together, encouraged, and supported each other. There was a spirit of 'We're in this together,' and the atmosphere was incredibly positive. My conclusion is: Even in the best market times, if relationships are sour, life is sour. But even in the worst market times, if relationships are good, life is good." The same can be said for families, churches, and any other organization.

The different personalities have different communication styles and different needs in relationships:

Missouris value action more than discussion. They tend to use people to accomplish their goals. They want relationships that are based on doing something constructive together.

Paradise Stars enjoy a lot of people and a lot of variety. They want a multitude of "best friends" who don't demand too much of them. If they feel pressured, they quickly move to spend time with another friend.

Intrepids want a few, deep friendships with loyal, reflective people. They get their feelings hurt easily, and they wilt under criticism. They want a safe, supportive environment so they can relax and develop intimacy with another person.

Calypsos value relationships that are orderly and definable. They can be bullied, but they also may respond in open defiance. They want to know what is expected of them so they can meet those expectations.

Strive to understand the person with whom you are building a relationship. Don't assume people are like you.

They probably aren't! And don't demand that they treat you a certain way. Learn to value their attempts (any attempts!) to move toward you, but also communicate your needs and desires for the relationship. Somewhere in the middle is love and understanding.

Develop Spiritual Strength

In the past 20 years, a spiritual awakening has been sweeping our country. People are more open to spiritual matters today than ever before. Walk in any bookstore and you will see a multitude of books about God, spirituality, and angels. Unfortunately, much of the interest is amorphous, formless spiritualism. People thirst for God. That's good. But they are trying to drink from fountains which may not be able to quench that thirst. I am thankful, however, that so many people from all walks of life sense the need for meaning beyond themselves.

We can look to God for wisdom. He is the Creator, and He knows how things are supposed to work! The principles we find in the Bible provide guidance for decision-making. It's all there. We just need to read and apply those principles.

We can look to God for purpose. God loves us more than we can possibly comprehend, and He has a plan for each of us that is beyond our wildest imaginations. He wants us to experience His gracious presence and feel His strong hand guiding us.

We can look to God for strength. Throughout the pages of the Bible and the annals of church history, men and women looked to God in times of trouble. When all hope was lost, God gave hope and direction. Even in the darkest hours, He made Himself known to people. Corrie ten Boom and her sister endured the horrors of the Nazi's Ravensbruck concentration camp. When her sister wanted to give up the struggle to live, Corrie told her, "There is no pit so deep that God is not deeper still."

Our view of God shapes our response to Him. Many of us have significant misunderstandings about the character of God. Perhaps we didn't have a loving, strong father to model the nature of God to us, and we find it difficult to believe that God is so kind and gracious. Understanding the character of God requires pursuit and effort, like mining for gold. We find a few nuggets on the top, and those encourage us that there is more—much more—below the surface. As we dig, we uncover rich veins of the riches of His love and purpose for us.

God has gone to great lengths to help us understand what He is like. He has given us a wealth of insights in the Scriptures about His character. The Bible has many names for God which describe specific elements of His nature and how we relate to Him. Three of them are most significant:

• *Elohim* signifies that He is a creative God. He spoke and a billion galaxies were flung into the heavens. He formed you and me—with enough beauty to appreciate His care and with a blemish or two to keep us humble.

• *Jehovah* is the name for God that refers to the covenant relationship He has with His people. He has made a firm commitment to me as my Father and my God, and I in turn have responded in making a commitment to Him. As a friend of mine said, "It isn't as important that I am grasping His hand as it is that He is grasping mine."

• *Adonai* means "God is our Master and we are His servants." This may or may not sound all that attractive to those of us who have grown up in a free democracy, but it meant a lot to the children of Israel. One of my favorite passages of the Bible is Exodus 21. In that culture, if a man owed money and could not pay his debt, he became an indentured servant. After he had worked the prescribed number of years, he was set free. If the master has been loving and kind, however, the servant might choose to stay. Moses stated,

> But if the servant declares, 'I love my master and my wife and children and do not want to go free,' then his master must take him before the judges. He shall take him to the door or the doorpost and pierce his ear with an awl. Then he will be his servant for life. (Exodus 21:5-6)

From that day on, everyone would see the hole in the man's ear and know that he could be free, but he responded to the kindness of his master and chose to stay. That is a wonderful picture of our response to the love of God. We are free to leave, but we choose to remain in His service because He loves us so much.

These three names of God are found in the Old Testament. The prophets told of one who would come who would be God in the flesh, the Messiah who would die to pay for mankind's sins. That one is Jesus Christ. The writer to the Hebrews said that Jesus is the "exact representation" of the God of the Old Testament (Hebrews 1:3). As God in the flesh, He is Elohim, Jehovah, and Adonai.

So . . . how do we know what God is like? We look at Jesus Christ. How do we develop spiritual strength? By loving Him with all our hearts and pursuing Him and His purposes in our lives.

See Life as an Adventure!

We have a choice to make every day. We can see life as a wonderful adventure, or we can see it as a painful drudgery. We can wake up and say, "Good morning, Lord!" or we can wake up and moan, "Good Lord, morning." Same words—different attitude. Our attitude becomes a self-fulfilling prophesy for good or ill. If we look forward to enjoying the day, we will almost always find people and situations to enjoy. But if we dread each tick of the foreboding clock, we will find only obstacles, heartache, and despair. If we have an optimistic, adventuresome spirit, there's no telling what we can find along life's way.

The little freckle-faced shepherd boy David was told by his dad to take cheese to his brothers in the army with King Saul. David grabbed a sack of groceries and headed out. He had no idea of the incredible adventure that awaited him that day.

When he arrived, the army was in a panic. A giant named Goliath, over nine feet tall, stood on the plain in front of them yelling for anyone in the army of God to come fight him. For 39 days, Goliath had yelled insults, and the Israelites only looked at each other and winced. David heard the giant's taunts, and he determined to kill him.

David? Kill the giant? He wasn't a soldier. He'd never been trained in combat. And he was just a kid. What business did he have taking the challenge when combat-hardened soldiers quaked in their boots (or sandals)? These men had listened to the giant day after day. They saw how big he was and how mean he looked. They focused on the problem. But David focused on God and the possibility.

What went through David's mind as he made his momentous decision to fight Goliath? He remembered his experience when he was alone on the hillside and his flock of sheep was attacked by a lion and a bear. There was no army to help him. Only God. David took action and killed both animals. If God could help him protect some insignificant sheep, couldn't God help him kill Israel's enemy?

David asked, "What will be done for the man who kills this Philistine and removes this disgrace from Israel?" They told him that Saul would give the man great wealth. He would also give the man his daughter in marriage and exempt his father's family from taxes. To be sure, David said to them, "Run that by me again." He had them repeat the promises so he would be sure the benefits at least matched the risks. Bucks, a babe, and no taxes. Cool! Bring on the big fella!

Saul was willing for David to try. In some ways, it was a tremendous risk for Saul to entrust his kingdom to a cocky kid, but then again, nobody else was willing to try. Goliath had immense armor, a gigantic sword, and a spear with a shaft as large as a weaver's beam. He was ready to rumble! Saul tried to fit his huge armor on David's frail frame, but it wouldn't work. He removed the armor and wore only his shepherd's garb. Then he picked up five smooth stones and ran toward the giant.

Saul thought Goliath was too big to hit. David thought he was too big to miss. David took out a stone, put it in his sling, and let it fly! ZZZZZZZZAP! Right in the forehead! Goliath fell in a heap. David grabbed the giant's sword and cut off his head. The Israelite soldiers attacked the fleeing Philistines and won the battle!

Did you notice that David took five stones, not just one? We find out later that Goliath had four brothers, just as big and bad as he was. David was ready. His attitude was, "I can lick you and your ugly brothers, too!"

Goliath was called "a champion." A champion is "one who rules the open places." Goliath was between the Israelites and where God wanted them to be. All of us have champions in our lives that will claim every inch of territory we let them have. They take the form of surly business associates, a grouchy spouse, a difficult relationship with a demanding parent or child, health concerns, procrastination, past failures, secrets, unresolved bitterness, and a host of others.

David hit Goliath in the forehead with the stone, then cut off his head. It's not enough to knock your problems down, you have to cut off their heads. Lots of times we make a dent in our "champion," but we fail to finish it off. We need to follow David's example to finish what we start and not let there be any substitute for a complete victory over our selfishness, laziness, or the effects of fear and hurt.

Some day in eternity, I believe God will show us our lives from His perspective. We will see the way He orchestrated events and people to provide opportunities for us to live full, happy lives. Every day can be a great adventure if we open our eyes to the challenges and serendipitous opportunities He places before us.

Take advantage of those opportunities. Make your life count. Leave a lasting legacy. God uses the ordinary to do extraordinary things. That's the real North Star—living for a cause greater than yourself. Teddy Roosevelt once said, "No man is worth his salt who is not ready at all times to risk his body, to risk his well-being, to risk his life, in a great cause." Throughout his life, TR risked his life and reputation over and over again for what he believed. He lived life to the fullest! We can, too.

Roles and Goals

Our roles are more important than our goals. When our goals conflict with our roles, our integrity suffers. For instance, being a husband and father are the most important roles in my life, and I don't let anything supersede these commitments. Several years ago, I was connected with an organization. Quite often, the leadership team talked about priorities. One day, the boss turned to me and said, "Why do you always bring our discussions back to your wife and daughters? It's getting a little old!"

"Because that's what I value most," I replied. "Their welfare is what determines my goals and schedule."

He didn't think much of my answer, and as time went on, it was obvious that he thought I should place a higher value on the success of the organization than on my family. That proved to be an unworkable situation for me, so I left the organization. It wasn't a difficult choice, even though I knew I would miss some of the people and the opportunities. I knew what I valued, and I wasn't going to change that.

In his book, *The Man in the Mirror*, Patrick Morley tells the story of a dentist and his 12-year-old son who went fishing in Alaska. The guide landed the float plane on a shoal in the river, but the water level went down and they couldn't take off until the next day. Overnight, a tiny hole in one of the pontoons allowed the rising water to fill up the pontoon. When they tried to take off the next day, the plane barely got airborne. When the extra weight made it crash in the middle of the river. The pilot and another man swam for safety. The current was strong. The boy couldn't make it. The father was a strong swimmer. He could have easily made the shore by himself, but he chose to stay with his son. As the pilot watched from dry ground, the father used a pair of waders as an air pocket to keep afloat. The last thing the pilot saw was the father putting his arms around his son as the current swept them toward the sea. In the cold water, hypothermia would overcome them in only a few minutes. The man could have lived, but his role as father was more important to him than anything in the world—even life itself.

Every loving father would do that for his son. Morely wonders: *If all of us would be willing to die for our families, why aren't we all willing to live for them? Why don't we pursue lives that are worth our children emulating?*

❏ What does it mean for you to "embrace risk as a way of life"? In what ways do you need to be more cautious? In what ways do you need to be bolder?

❏ What are some reasons it is difficult for us to take responsibility for our feelings, attitudes, choices, and behaviors?

❏ How do you feel around demanding people? Explain:

❏ Are you a demanding person? Why or why not?

❏ Why is it easier to wear a mask than to be real?

❏ Look at the list of masks in this chapter. Which of these are present in your life? What do you gain by wearing each one? What do you lose?

❏ Look at the Feelings Word List. Which of these emotions have you experienced in the past 24 hours?

❏ Which emotions (list 4 to 6) do you experience most often?

❑ Explain the correlation between purpose and personal growth.

❑ What interests keep you learning and growing right now?

❑ What do you want to "dive into" in the future? What do you hope to gain from these new insights and skills?

❑ Think of the best friends you've ever had. Describe what those relationships were like.

❑ Make a list of your friends. What is the personality type of each one?

❑ How can you be a better friend to each of them?

❑ Has your relationship with your earthly father shaped your view of your heavenly Father? If so, explain how.

❏ Describe your relationship with God. (What about Him encourages you? What discourages you? What gives you peace? What produces guilt?)

❏ At what points in your life have you been most optimistic and adventuresome? Describe those times.

❏ On a scale of 0 (nada) to 10 (totally), rate how you are doing in applying each of these principles to your life:

—Embrace risk as a way of life

0   1   2   3   4   5   6   7   8   9   10

—Take responsibility

0   1   2   3   4   5   6   7   8   9   10

—Be honest about your emotions

0   1   2   3   4   5   6   7   8   9   10

—Never stop learning

    0   1   2   3   4   5   6   7   8   9   10

—Value meaningful relationships

    0   1   2   3   4   5   6   7   8   9   10

—Develop spiritual strength

    0   1   2   3   4   5   6   7   8   9   10

—See life as an adventure!

    0   1   2   3   4   5   6   7   8   9   10

❏ The one principle I want to focus on in the coming days is:

And I hope the results are:

8
PRIORITIES: DREAMS UNDER CONSTRUCTION

Don't be afraid to dream. Physicist Albert Einstein said, "When I examine myself and my methods of thought, I come to the conclusion that the gift of fantasy has meant more to me than my talent for absorbing positive knowledge." Dreams drive brilliant minds, and they give life to the rest of us as well.

Robert Fulghum tells a great story about a truck driver named Larry Walters. All his life, Larry had wanted to fly. He had dreamed of soaring over the housetops in his Los Angeles neighborhood. One day, he decided to make his dream a reality. He took his aluminum lawn chair and tied 45, helium-filled, surplus weather balloons to it. He hooked on a parachute, a CB radio, a six-pack of beer, some PB&J sandwiches, and a pellet gun so he could pop some balloons and descend when he wanted to.

Larry expected to coast just above the houses and fly eye-level with the birds, but in only a few minutes his location was reported by a plane landing at LAX. When Walters was at 12,860 feet, he found out his pellet gun wasn't powerful enough to penetrate the balloons! After a long time in the air, he finally floated down to earth . . . into the waiting arms of police.

Eager reporters asked Walters two questions: "What was it like?" and "Will you ever do it again?" Larry shrugged, "You can't just sit there." He was asked if he would do it again, and he said, "Nope." When he was asked if he was glad he had done it, he grinned and said, "Oh, yes!"

Dreams give us life and vitality. They are the driving force behind the North Star Principles. If we don't dream, we're almost dead already. Of course, we can always find people who will tell us our dreams are silly or insignificant. Those are the people whose spirits have been dead for years.

Everyone has a dream. We may be pursuing it with all our hearts, or we may have buried it and forgotten about it. Great people have great dreams. Fulfilling those dreams is what makes them great. But common people have dreams, too. Setting a high goal and going for it makes us alive. Our senses are on edge. Relationships are more meaningful. We notice more. We hope more intensely. But dreams also have a price tag. Just ask Joan of Arc, or ask Martin Luther King. Ask millions of men and women who have cared deeply about a cause. And sometimes our hopes and dreams simply fail. That hurts. I am reminded of King Solomon's trenchant comment: "Hope deferred makes the heart sick, but a longing fulfilled is a tree of life" (Proverbs 13:12).

When you and I are tempted to gripe and whine and give up trying, we should think of Helen Keller. This remarkable woman overcame the incredible obstacles of being blind, deaf, and mute to live a full and purposeful life. She said, "Security is mostly a superstition. It does not exist in nature, nor do the children of men as a whole experience it. Avoiding danger is no safer in the long run than outright exposure. Life is either a daring adventure or nothing." If Helen Keller can reach her dreams, you and I can, too.

What happens when we are married to someone who is a cynical dream-killer? We may stay strong for a while, but sooner or later, the dream erodes under the constant friction of doubt and criticism. Solomon, the wise king who knew a lot about women, wrote about the problem of living with someone who drains your hope and enthusiasms: "Better to live on a corner of the roof than share a house with a quarrelsome wife" (Proverbs 21:9). And that goes both ways!

I Want My Girls to Know . . .

One of the things that has helped me prioritize my life is to consider: *What do I want my daughters, Abigail and Danielle, to know today if I'm not here tomorrow?* Answering this question exposes and shapes my values. In responding, I realize what I value most are faith, family, and friends. I have always liked this little poem. It reflects my own commitments.

> People use all types of yardsticks to measure success—
> money, houses, cars, awards, status—
> but the measure of real success is one you can't spend.
> It's the way your child describes you when talking to a friend.

Here are the things I want to be sure my daughters know (and of course, they will only know these things if I model them instead of just mouthing them):

About me:
- I love you very much!
- I am so proud to be your father!
- I would gladly die for you!
- There is nothing you can do that will cause me to stop loving you. I may not like your actions, but I will always love you!

Socially:
- Be a lady at all times.
- Be a leader, not just a follower. (Know when it's right to be a leader and when to be a follower.)
- Do what is right and not what is easy.
- Keep yourself sexually pure.
- If you marry, choose a man who is a spiritual leader.
- Choose your friends slowly and be even slower to leave them.
- Seek to understand and don't demand to be understood.

Attitude:
- Be positive, hopeful, and expectant.
- Believe God for great things.
- Love God with all your heart.
- Believe in yourself.
- Believe in others.

Personal accountability:
- Always do your best.
- Hard work will always precede rewards.
- Give, and it will be given unto you.
- Always give more than you take.
- Take responsibility for your behavior. Don't blame others.
- You have the ability to choose, but you can't choose the consequences.

- Your choices today will determine your lifestyle tomorrow.
- If you can make the choice, God can make the change.
- Value the right things: money is a good servant but a poor master.

Mentally:
- Be a lifelong learner.
- Study for knowledge, not a diploma or a degree.
- Learn to love books.

Vision:
- Don't be afraid to dream.
- Set clear, written, concise goals.
- Begin with the end in mind.
- A winner is someone who gets up one more time than he or she has been knocked down.
- Never doubt in the dark what you know is true in the light.

And finally:
- Have fun!
- Never teach a pig to sing. It will only waste your time and just annoy the pig!
- I love you more than you can know!

Your Purpose Statement

One of the most important things you can do—and perhaps the most important thing that will come out of this book for you—is to create your own purpose statement. There are several ways people find focus for their lives. Some are good ways; some aren't so good:
- We can let other people tell us what we should do with our lives. That's not a bad thing when we are five years old and want to run out into the street without

looking, but as adults, we have the responsibility to chart our own course.

• We can be squeezed into a mold by circumstances. If your dad owns a business and wants you to take it over from him, should you do it? If the only job you can find is one that seems like a dead-end for you, should you take it? If your health deteriorates, will your purpose in life change?

• We can emulate others. A parent, sibling or friend may live an attractive, successful life, and we may want to be just like this person.

• We can react to others' failures. Instead of emulating someone, we can recoil from their out-of-control, destructive lifestyles and choose to be as different as possible.

In different ways, all of these have some merit. We need to listen to other people, observe their successes, learn from their failures, and be open to needs. But all of these ultimately allow others to determine the direction and meaning of our lives.

• We can think, pray, and reflect to discover what is the guiding purpose of our lives. It becomes our purpose statement, not someone else's, and it shapes our commitments, goals, and relationships.

• We can spend time with wise men and women who can give us feedback on our mission in life.

• We can take steps to fulfill our sense of mission and see if there is a "sense of rightness" about our direction.

Here are some principles to help you discover your North Star purpose statement:

1. Determining your purpose is a spiritual experience.

Our sense of purpose is derived from the deepest parts of our souls. It is based on ethics, morals, and values which are actually spiritual principles.

2. Your purpose shapes your goals.

Goals change. You might want to buy a bigger house or go on vacation or make a specific contribution to someone's life, but these usually are accomplished (or perhaps not), and then you move on to other goals. Your purpose is the highest calling, your passion, your driving force that gives you perspective to allow you to say "yes" to some goals and "no" to others.

3. Your purpose shapes your relationships.

We can either use people or love them. If our purpose is honorable and unselfish, we will be givers, not takers. We will value love, honesty, and genuine commitments through the ups and downs of every relationship.

4. Your purpose will probably remain constant throughout your life, but it may be refined from time to time.

As we mature and go through life's experiences, we gain a clearer understanding of what our lives mean and how we can have a positive impact on others. We may find our purpose evolves over time, and it becomes clearer and clearer as we experience fulfillment in influencing others' lives and reaching important goals.

5. You need the honest feedback of others to sharpen your purpose.

We all need a mentor or at least the honest appraisal of someone who has been around the block a few times so we can check ourselves to see if we are on the right path. For instance, if someone believes she is to be the leader in a great social cause but has never led anything before, she might need to be redirected a bit. Her purpose of advancing the cause may be laudable, but her role in advancing it may need to be adjusted.

6. Your actions need to be consistent with your words.

If we say our family is most important but spend 70 to 80 hours a week at work with precious little energy left for our spouse and children, we are grossly inconsistent. Some of us are quite skilled in convincing ourselves that we are doing all this for our families, but that's where we need a wise and trusted friend to observe our lives and speak the truth—however painful it may be—to us.

Four Questions

Rick Warren is the pastor of Saddleback Valley Community Church in Orange County, California, which is one of the most successful church starts in Southern Baptist history. He is the author of the excellent book, *The Purpose-Driven Church.* In a tape series, Warren lists four questions which help people determine their purpose in life. These are:

#1 What will be the center of my life?

We may choose a career, status, possessions, power, money, family, friendships, or God to be the hub of our life's wheel, but we need to be very careful to put something or someone worthy in that important position.

#2 What will be the character of my life?

Under the smiles and facades, under the masks and white lies, what is inside you and me? Character is far more important than any riches and prestige we can ever have, now and for eternity. God will take us through all kinds of difficulties to prune away the excesses of selfishness and pride until our character is refined. The problem, of course, is that we often get angry and confused because we want comfort and affluence, not a refined character. Can you tell if someone has been refined in that way? I sure can. The person exhibits the attractive attributes of humility, honesty, patience, and love.

#3 What will be the contribution of my life?

Each of us is given a wealth of "capital" in life: time, talent, riches, and relationships. At the end of our lives, an accounting will occur. Actually, there will be two. As family and friends stand at our graveside, they will reflect on how we influenced them—for good or ill. Some will speak their accounting to those standing nearby; others will simply figure the ledger sheet in their heads without saying a word. I want those people standing at my grave to say, "Ike made a difference in my life. I'm so thankful I knew him." Another accounting will take place "on the other side." Each of us will stand before God and He will ask two questions: "What did you do with Jesus Christ? And what did you do with all I gave you?" Our answers to those questions will make a difference for us in eternity.

#4 What will be the communication of my life?

What is your cause, your life's message? What makes you shout? What makes your blood boil in anger? What issue burns in you that you have to tell people—no, *convince* people—so they understand what you understand and feel what you feel? Some of us used to have a passion like this, but years of too many hours at work and demands at home have left us numb and uncaring. I'll bet that spark is still there. I'll bet even reading these words has awakened memories of times when you really cared about something so passionately that you couldn't wait to talk to people about it.

But some of us are so hot-tempered that we communicate passionately about too many things—and our passion is focused on our own comfort, prestige, power, and selfishness. Not a pretty picture! Our life's message should be outside ourselves. It should be concerned with the welfare of others so that it moves our hearts like no other issue in the world.

In a now legendary conversation, Steve Jobs, the founder of Apple Computer, tried to recruit John Sculley, the president of Pepsi, to be the president of Apple. Sculley couldn't understand why he should leave his prestigious and powerful position at Pepsi to work for Apple. "Why should I leave Pepsi for Apple Computer?" Sculley asked. Jobs looked at Sculley and said, "Do you want to spend the rest of your life selling sugared water, or do you want to change the world?"

How will you and I change the world (or at least the corner of it where we live)? That's what purpose is all about.

Create Your Own Purpose Statement

❏ Take plenty of time to be alone to think and pray about your purpose statement. Read the paragraphs under each question in this section about creating your purpose statement to stimulate and clarify your thinking. Write your responses to the following questions. Don't rush through this! Allow thoughts to come to you. Think of additional questions you want to consider and experiences you have enjoyed.

#1 What will be the center of my life?

#2 What will be the character of my life?

#3 What will be the contribution of my life?

#4 What will be the communication of my life?

❑ Based on your reflection on these four questions, write a brief, poignant purpose statement. (You may want to write it several times over the next few days until you have one that "captures" your heart.)

❑ Share your purpose statement with several people and tell them why you are excited about it.

Image or Substance?

Some of us have lived for someone else's purposes. They have played the tune and we danced! And some of us have played a role all our lives and haven't been ourselves. One of the most significant lessons we can learn in life is to stop living other people's dreams and find our own. Now, don't get me wrong. I'm not advocating a selfish dream. I'm advocating one that you can embrace wholeheartedly and independently. In fact, God can be the source of our dreams. One man told me, "True success is finding what God wants you to do and then doing it with all your heart." Not a bad idea!

❏ What are your dreams? What turns your crank? Take some time to think about what you dream in each of the following areas. (Use extra paper if necessary.)

—Purpose
My dream is:

—Marriage
My dream is:

—Children
My dream is:

—Career
My dream is:

—Finances
My dream is:

—Health
My dream is:

—Relationship with God
My dream is:

—Hobbies and leisure
My dream is:

—Lifestyle
My dream is:

—Identity (How you think about yourself)
My dream is:

❏ For each of these categories, determine the tension between others' expectations and your dreams.

—Purpose

Others expect:

The tension I feel is:

—Marriage

Others expect:

The tension I feel is:

—Children
Others expect:

The tension I feel is:

—Career
Others expect:

The tension I feel is:

—Finances
Others expect:

The tension I feel is:

—Health
Others expect:

The tension I feel is:

—Relationship with God
Others expect:

The tension I feel is:

—Hobbies and leisure
Others expect:

The tension I feel is:

—Lifestyle
Others expect:

The tension I feel is:

—Identity (How you think about yourself)
Others expect:

The tension I feel is:

❑ Summarize your conclusions about your dreams, others' expectations, and the tension between the two. Which area produces the least tension? Which area produces the most? What can you do to resolve that tension?

9
THE LADDER OF INTIMACY

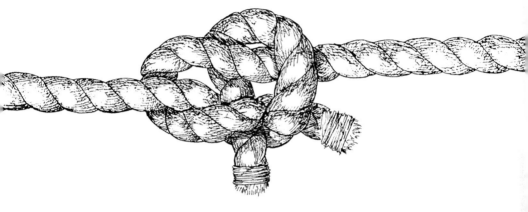

Communication is part art, part science, and part instinct. We can craft beautiful words to share our love with someone, but there is also an art to effective confrontation. The science of communication is the study of the intricate interplay of verbal and nonverbal messages to different personality types, but most of us rely on instinct to know how much to tell someone about ourselves. In our conversations, we take a small step. If that step is secure, we may choose to take the next one. Each of these takes us higher on the ladder of intimacy and enables us to fulfill the North Star Principle of valuing meaningful relationships.

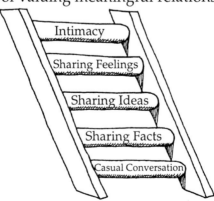

First Rung: Casual Conversation

The first rung is what we say to people to "break the ice." We are in line at the bank, and we say to the person behind us, "This line sure is slow." We walk past an acquaintance in the parking lot, and we say, "Hi. How's it going?" All we expect to hear is the usual, "Fine. How are you?" This is "elevator-speak." We don't expect more and, in fact, we don't want more.

Second Rung: Sharing Facts

With acquaintances, co-workers, friends, and family members, we often begin our conversations with sharing facts. We comment on the weather, the time of day, how busy we've been, the stock market, a news event, and almost anything under the sun. If that exchange is met with warmth and acceptance, we might choose to go to the next level.

Third Rung: Sharing Ideas

The first two steps aren't much of a risk unless you happen to share facts with an enraged rhino. (I know a few of those who wear pants or skirts!) The third rung, however, contains the first real risk factor: the sharing of ideas. If we can defend our ideas successfully, or if we are sure the other person will accept whatever we say, then we will proceed at this level. The vast majority of male friendships are based on shared ideas about politics, sports, business, and women.

Fourth Rung: Sharing Feelings

Men may communicate that they are angry about anything and everything, but they seldom get below the surface anger to the deeper feelings. At this level, we share the hurts, fears, happiness, and joys of life. Tears and laughter may occasionally be expressed at the lower rungs, but this is where they are at home. Women build friendships at this level most frequently.

Fifth Rung: Intimacy

Transparency is the hallmark of an intimate relationship. The masks come off for two reasons: they aren't needed, and they aren't tolerated. People on the fifth rung share their dreams and dreads, their deepest secrets and their greatest hopes. Open, honest communication surfaces any problems, and these problems are resolved to protect the cherished depth of the relationship.

As we move up the ladder, there are fewer and fewer people on each rung. Trust is the necessary component for each person to take the next step up the ladder. Some of us trust very easily (some, too easily!), and for a variety of reasons, some of us refuse to trust even if the other person has proven he or she is trustworthy. Most of us, however, will respond when and if we are convinced the other person has our best interests at heart.

Be patient with yourself and others as you seek to take the next step. Don't push. Instead, address the issue of trust as the foundation of progress, and be trustworthy so your friend or partner will feel safe enough to take the next step.

Of course, intimacy is not the goal of every relationship. It is the goal of marriages and family relationships, and perhaps a few friendships, but it is probably not wise to try to reach that level of communication at work. Job relationships have a different set of rules. Job performance and profitability are the goals, not intimacy. Don't demand it there, and if someone expects it of you, gently back off from these expectations.

Steps Up the Ladder

As we are aware of these rungs in the ladder of intimacy, we can take specific steps to take our conversations—and our relationships—to the next level. Some of those steps include:

Listening

Sometimes we are too stubborn to be good listeners. A battleship was maneuvering through a night storm just off the coast. Someone on the ship's bridge saw a light in the distance, and the admiral on board sent the message, "You are in our course. Turn left eight degrees."

The reply came back, "No, *you* turn *right* eight degrees."

The admiral angrily despatched the message, "I am the admiral of the fleet. Turn left eight degrees at once!"

The approaching light responded, "This is the lighthouse. Turn right eight degrees."

One of the ways I know if I am really listening to someone is if I am asking follow-up questions. If I'm not, I'm probably thinking about the next very clever thing I plan to say, or I may simply not be interested in what the other person is talking about.

Eye contact is essential to good listening. We "listen with our eyes" when we give a person our total attention. This is particularly difficult with small children who want to talk endlessly after we've had a hard day. It takes a supreme effort to focus on that child's stream of thought (or lack of same) and ask follow-up questions. But it means the world to that child!

Sometimes, if we think somebody has tuned us out, we can ask forthrightly, "Are you listening to me?" (I've wanted to ask, "What was the last sentence I said?" but I didn't want to hear the person say, "Duhh, you mean after you said 'Hello'?")

Listening is hard work. It requires a commitment to "be fully there" for the other person. Sometimes what the person says is interesting to us; sometimes not. But it is almost always interesting to them, and if we love them, we'll pay attention.

Affirming

In a national park in the west, the park rangers noticed over several years that the population of wild horses was flourishing but the population of wild donkeys was decreasing. As government agencies do, they launched a full scale investigation of the situation. After careful, painstaking analysis, they found that when horses were attacked by the wolves in the park area, the horses formed a defensive circle by putting their heads together and kicking at the wolves. The donkeys, however, panicked. They got in a clump and kicked each other! The ones injured by their own kind were then devoured by the wolves. So do we want to act like horses or donkeys? We have a choice.

Why is it that we notice and verbalize the bad things we see in other people but seldom notice and verbalize the *good* we see in them? Are we afraid they will get cocky? Are we jealous of the attention? It does other people a world of good for us to point out their positive character traits, the skills they have developed, and the contributions they have made. And our words just may return to us in the form of affirmation, too.

Some people are hard to affirm. They are crusty, belligerent, thankless, critical old bags! (There, I said it! I feel better.) Look beyond the crustiness and see the good in others . . . including the defiant teenager who lives under your roof, or your quarrelsome spouse, or your demanding boss, or your "nothing-ever-works-out-for-me" friend. Words of affirmation change the climate in a room . . . and in a relationship.

Forgiving

When someone has hurt us, everything in us cries out for revenge, but we will settle for justice. The desire for justice is a part of our human nature. It is built-in equipment. Forgiveness is foreign to us. In an article a few years ago, author Phillip Yancey called forgiveness "the unnatural act." I think he's right.

Too often, we confuse excusing with forgiving. We say, "Oh, he couldn't help it," or "She didn't really mean what she said." But the wound remains, unbandaged and unforgiven . . . and it festers. Some have said, "Don't forgive until he asks for it" or " . . . until she's really sorry for what she did." But forgiveness is for our benefit to free us from the gnawing resentment and bitterness that eats away our sense of love and prevents us from enjoying life.

The Bible describes forgiveness in two ways. In Romans 12, Paul says forgiveness is not taking revenge . . . that it is choosing not to exact justice on the person or even to gossip about the offense to others. Paul goes one step further and instructs us to feed our enemy and give a drink of water to those who have hurt us. (Romans 12:20) How can we have this attitude? Because we can be supremely confident that God's justice will ultimately prevail. Paul reminds us: "Do not take revenge, my friends, but leave room for God's wrath, for it is written: 'It is mine to avenge; I will repay,' says the Lord" (Romans 12:19). We can leave it in God's strong, just hands.

Another picture of forgiveness is found in Matthew's Gospel. In chapter 18, Peter asked Jesus a question: "Lord, how many times shall I forgive my brother when he sins against me? Up to seven times?" Jesus replied, "I tell you, not seven times, but seventy-seven times" (Matthew 18:21-22). Jesus then told a parable about a servant who owed his king an incredible amount of money, the equivalent of billions of dollars today. His debt was so great, he had no chance to repay it. The king graciously forgave the man and cancelled the debt. End of story? No, the man didn't understand that he was forgiven. He found a fellow servant who owed him a little money. When this man couldn't repay his debt, the first servant's anger overcame him, and he choked the man. When we fail to realize the forgiveness we have received from God for our debts, we try to extract payment from other people who have offended us. To the extent that we grasp the incredible forgiveness of God for our own sins, we will be quick to forgive others.

Paul described this spiritual principle in two of his letters. To the Ephesians he wrote, "Be kind and compassionate to one another, forgiving each other, just as in Christ God forgave you" (Ephesians 4:32). If we are having a difficult time forgiving someone, we need to focus first on Christ's forgiveness of us. Then we will be able to share that wealth with others.

Forgiveness, however, is not the same as reconciliation. Forgiveness is unilateral. We can choose to forgive whether the other person repents or not, whether the person is sorry or not, whether the person makes amends or not, and whether the person even acknowledges guilt or not. But reconciliation takes two. Both parties must be willing to take steps toward each other, to forgive and to repent, to rebuild broken trust a step at a time. Quite often, only one party is willing to take those steps. We can't control that other person. He makes his own choices, and sometimes those choices hurt us again. And we forgive again.

When we choose to forgive, we may feel a great sense of relief . . . or we may feel a deep sense of sadness. Forgiveness, especially of severe offenses, involves grieving the losses and wounds we have experienced. Anger is often a component of that grief. Don't wait to forgive until you feel peaceful and happy toward that person. Remember that forgiveness is "an unnatural act." Make that hard choice and free yourself from the bondage of bitterness.

Forgiveness is a great gift to give each other in a family. When I mess up (which unfortunately is fairly frequently), Robin, Abigail, and Danielle are quick to forgive. They'll never know how much that means to me.

Speaking Truth

Misunderstandings can cause a lot of anxiety. The entire British nation anxiously awaited word about the battle. General Wellington had entered battle against Napoleon's legions which had swept across Europe for the past several years. The battle at Waterloo ebbed and flowed but at the end of the day, Wellington's Redcoats had beaten the French. As the fog rolled in, a courier was sent to the coast to send a message across the English Channel. On the English side, they saw only the first two words of the cryptic, three-word message: WELLINGTON DEFEATED. As word spread across England, the people were devastated at the army's tragedy. The next morning as sun burned off the fog, the rest of the message was seen: WELLINGTON DEFEATED NAPOLEON, and a sigh of relief was heard just before the cries of rejoicing in Great Britain.

Many times the problem isn't the misunderstanding of hearing something that wasn't communicated; the problem is dishonesty. Lies take on many forms. We can create an outright fabrication of truth, but more often, we exaggerate, making good things a little better and bad things a little worse. Why do we do that? To impress people a little more or win a little more sympathy. When we exaggerate in gossip, the motive is revenge, to hurt that person we are talking about. Another form of dishonesty is keeping secrets from those who need to know the truth. An employee may know about a friend's embezzlement, but he acts like he doesn't know a thing when the auditor asks questions. Some families play the painful and destructive game of talking *about* a person but not *to* that person. For instance, they may endlessly discuss a family member's problem with debt, drinking, gambling, anger, or any of a host of other difficulties, but they never talk directly to that person to confront the issue and find a workable solution.

Truth is sometimes affirming; sometimes it is corrective. It should always be spoken with the good of the other person in mind. That means we should be selective in how we communicate the truth and how much of the truth we communicate. When a wife asks her husband, "How do I look in my new dress?" the truth may be that she would look better if she lost 20 pounds, but it is more prudent to say something like, "It is a beautiful dress, dear. I really like it." Paul encourages us to "speak the truth in love" (Ephesians 4:15). That simple statement gives us a directive, but with boundaries. We are to speak the truth, but our motives should always be encouragement, affirmation, loving correction, and restoration.

Confronting with Kindness

Battleships and research vessels don't mind pointing out the shortcomings of others, but they hate to have their own errors in the glare of the spotlight. Cruise ships and sailboats don't want anything to rock the boat. They'd rather talk about other things than problems between them and others. In those rare times that we need to confront others, we should temper it with kindness. Those of us who are sensitive and kind need to realize that if we love someone, we sometimes need to say hard things to them for their benefit.

Obviously there is a wide range of situations when we speak words of correction. Some are minor, and some are monumental. Here are some principles of confrontation which can be adapted to each situation:

1. Prepare—Missouris and Calypsos need to remind themselves that their goal is restoration and encouragement, not blasting the person into submission. Intrepids and Paradise Stars can remember that if they truly love people, they will take whatever steps are necessary to help others, including confronting them with the truth.

Ask God for wisdom and strength as you get ready to communicate. Write out what you want to say so you will be crystal clear. If the confrontation is a big deal, get the advice of a wise, competent counselor or friend who will give you objective, honest feedback. As you prepare, keep in mind:

- Avoid words like *always* and *never*.
- Don't bring up things the person had nothing to do with.
- Don't use humor to cover your pain.
- Don't let yourself be manipulated so that you give up or give in.

2. Major on the majors—Don't bring up the 473 ways the person has offended you in the past 37 years. There may be far more than that, but this isn't the time to create an index of all of them! Focus on one to three patterns or specific events. If the person responds well to these things, then you can move on to the next few in a few weeks or months.

3. Use *I* statements—Don't wade in accusingly by pointing your verbal finger in the person's face by saying, "You did this, and you did that! You are a miserable jerk!" That certainly will communicate, but it won't form the basis for understanding and reason! Instead, follow this formula of communicating: I feel. . . . I want. . . . I will. . . .

For example, a wife told her husband, "I feel hurt when you spend so much time at the office and are so tired when you come home that we can't talk. I want to spend quality time with you so our relationship will grow and deepen. I want you to come home by 6 o'clock at least one night during the week so we can have dinner and talk together. I will coordinate my schedule with yours to be sure we have that quality time together. If you don't make time for us to be together, I'll bring up the subject again and again. It's that important to me."

If the person says, "I don't care how you feel!" then you have a bigger problem on your hands. It is not a safe relationship. Focus then on the "I want" and "I will" statements and be as objective as possible. In business relationships, it is usually wise to avoid "I feel" statements altogether. Remember, the goals of business relationships are different from the goals of relationships with family and friends.

4. Be direct—That's no problem for battleships! But it can be a big problem for those of us whose brains turn to oatmeal when we are eyeball to eyeball in a confrontation. Keep the paper you wrote to prepare for the meeting, and pull it out to help you follow through with your goals for the conversation.

5. Anticipate the person's response and be prepared—How has this person previously responded to confrontation—in anger, self-pity, shifting the blame, withdrawal, or some other way that attempts to skirt the issue? Quite often, the

person will find plenty of excuses for his behavior and far too often, he will attack you for having the nerve to speak the truth. If you anticipate the response, you will be prepared so you can remain strong. It is a good idea to practice and get input from a counselor or pastor as you prepare so you can be ready for the person's reactions.

6. Clarify—Confrontation is difficult for both the confronter and the confronted. Minds race. Thoughts get confused. Attention wanders. Clarify what the other person is saying by restating his or her point: "This is what I hear you saying. Is that right?" And to be sure you are understood, ask questions like, "What did you hear me say?"

A very helpful technique to use in heated confrontations is to practice immediacy. When the conversation is overheated or out of control, stop and ask, "What is going on in this conversation right now?" I've seen many people talk to their spouse about an uncaring attitude, and when the spouse is confronted, he blows up and blames the other person. At that moment, you have a prime example right in front of you. Stop and say, "This is exactly what I'm talking about. I shared my hurt about you not caring for me, and you blow up and blame me. Do you see what I'm talking about now?"

7. Ask for a response—Your "I want" statement is a request for the other person to respond. It can be as simple as the desire for the person to let you finish your sentences before he interrupts, or it can be the requirement for marriage counseling if the relationship is to continue. Remember, however, that most people don't respond well in the heat of the moment. I suggest you give the person a day to think it over and then give you an answer.

A part of asking for a response is having consequences for failure to respond. Some of these are natural consequences like the continued erosion of trust, but other consequences can have to do with privileges, money, and in the business world, compensation and opportunities.

8. Take responsibility—Some of us are blame shifters: If there's a problem, it's always someone else's fault. In the confrontation, the person may tell you that you have hurt him in some way. Accept responsibility for your shortcomings, but be careful. Some of us are the opposite: blame sponges—we take responsibility for any and every problem, real and imagined. When a blame shifter tries to manipulate the sponge by accusing the sponge of hurting him, the sponge needs to stay strong and say, "I'm sorry I hurt you. Now I want to go back to the original point of how your anger has affected our relationship."

9. Stay strong—Some of us wilt after the confrontation is over. We feel we have given the supreme effort, and now we collapse. Follow through is just as important as preparation before the confrontation. Your plan needs to include how you will take specific steps to continue to communicate clearly, honestly, and regularly. It can also include specifics for implementing the consequences for the person's failure to respond.

10. Get help—If sharing your heart and communicating "I feel, I want, and I will" statements get you nowhere, call a pastor or counselor to help you sort out the strategy for taking the next step. In many cases, involving a professional counselor—or some other wise, objective third party—is the only way the other person will listen and have the motivation to change.

One of the things you will learn from the difficult exercise of confronting others is to take criticism graciously. If someone loves you enough to speak the truth in love to you, thank him for the depth of his concern. On the other hand, if someone is using angry confrontation to manipulate you, turn the tables on him and confront him about his attempt to control you. It is a wise person who knows the difference.

The Joy of Giving to Others

We can be so absorbed in our own priorities and busy schedules that we only bump into other people instead of genuinely loving and serving them. One of the great joys of life is giving time and attention to those we care about. Giving is contagious. The more we give, the more others give back to us. Our emotional tank is filled again by their love, and we have more to give. And the process continues to grow. The problem is that we expect others to give first. Sometimes they do. Many times they don't. Whether people give back to us now or much later, we are better people for getting out of ourselves and helping other people.

Some of us may choose to be a volunteer for a hospice or the Red Cross. Others will work on committees or in classes at church. But all of us can notice the people around us each day and give a pat on the back, open a door, and notice something someone did well.

Geese fly 70% further in a V-formation than if a single goose flies alone. In that formation, each goose takes his turn in the lead. The lead bird never honks. The others honk as encouragement to that lead goose so he will keep going strong.

In a NASCAR race, cars draft—follow one another very closely—to cut down on wind friction. I used to think it only helped the car in back, but a professional driver told me that drafting helps both cars go faster. That's why teammates draft each other so frequently.

Do you see others as competitors or partners? How we see them often determines how they act toward us. Missouris and Paradise Stars are naturally competitive and thrive on friendly competition. But Intrepids and Calypsos misunderstand that competitive zeal. They interpret it as manipulation and raw power to control others. Be sure you are communicating wisely to those around you. Don't assume they all see relationships as you do. They probably don't!

Biggies and Barriers

Professional counselors have noticed four issues that account for the vast majority of conflict in marriages: money, sex, children, and in-laws. Each of these can create tremendous stress for couples. They can drive the couple apart, or with patient communication and understanding, these issues can pull the couple together. For instance, it is very common for one parent to be strict and one to be lenient. If they resent the other's perspective on parenting, they attempt to undermine and counterbalance the situation.

For example, a child doesn't come home for dinner on time. One parent says to the child, "You knew when you were supposed to be home. No television for you tonight." The other interjects, "Wait a minute. He was only a few minutes late. He was playing with his friends and the time just slipped away. It's no big deal." If the parents don't come to an understanding about expectations and consequences—and how to enforce those—then everybody will lose. Each parent will try to protect the child from the "unfair" treatment of the other, and the poor child will be really confused! Similar conflicts about money, sex, and in-laws can create rifts—which become chasms—in the relationship.

The barriers to climbing the ladder of intimacy are legion. Some of us think we are too busy doing other things to carve out time for indepth communication. Many of us are so stressed out that all we can talk about are the pressing problems of today. We may be honest about those, but that doesn't build depth if that's all we ever talk about. We may have bad habits in lifestyle and communication. We may turn on the television or hide behind a book or magazine instead of engaging others in meaningful interaction. And the model of our families when we were children has profound effects on how we relate to others. If we saw our parents resolve problems effectively, we will probably acquire those skills as well, but if all we saw was rage or withdrawal (or both), then we will have a steeper hill to climb in developing good communication skills.

Personality and Communication

Several authors have identified different "languages" people use to communicate. If we speak the same language with another person, we will probably communicate well, but if we speak different languages, misunderstanding and confusion reign. Hurt and disillusionment follow soon after. Love, affirmation, and encouragement can come in many different forms. Here are a few:

words of affirmation
acts of kindness
meaningful touch
providing
protecting
being a companion
gifts
time

The four personality types tend to value particular modes of communicating love:

The Missouri communicates love by providing, protecting, and giving gifts. Battleships value love in action in return.

The Paradise Star communicates love by talking, touching, acts of kindness, and being a companion who is generous with his or her time. Cruise ships value these same things from others.

The Intrepid is the most sensitive. It communicates love in carefully crafted words of affirmation and acts of kindness. Sailboats take any criticism deeply to heart, so others need to couch their confrontations with gentleness. They give their time generously, and they expect others to give them plenty of time as well.

The Calypso communicates love in tangible ways of providing, protecting, and giving gifts. Research ships value orderly, active expressions of love in return.

Expectations: Realistic or Unrealistic?

In any relationship—family, business, or friendship—expectations determine the nature and direction of communication. If our expectations are realistic and well-founded, the relationship is much more likely to grow. When we have unrealistic expectations of one another—that is, we hope to get more than the other person can or will give—we are easily hurt, discouraged, and confused. Those feelings provide a very poor platform for progress in any relationship.

Others may have unrealistic expectations of us. Most often, these are unspoken so they are difficult to anticipate and resolve until some damage is done. For example:

• A woman from a divorced home marries a nice young man. He has no idea that she has a secret fear that he will leave her someday for some unknown reason. Her expectation is a negative one based on her past, and it can sabotage the relationship from the beginning if it is not addressed.

• An employer may meet a new employee and welcome the new person into the company. All the perks and benefits have been communicated to the new man on the team, but the Human Resources director failed to tell him that the boss expects each new person to put in 80 hours a week for the first year to prove his commitment to the company. When the boss explodes when he sees the new employee going home at 6 o'clock on Tuesday afternoon, the guy has no idea what the problem is. Again, if expectations are not clarified, the relationship will have some very rough sailing.

Once expectations are brought to light, then each person can make adjustments. They can communicate and compromise or part ways in some cases. That may be a far better solution in business relationships than continued confusion and pressure to live up to secret demands.

When I talk to couples about clarifying expectations of each other, sometimes I hear one say, "Well, I shouldn't have to say anything. If he were sensitive, he would already know what I need." Demanding that people read minds is another unrealistic expectation—and a pretty tall one at that! The first few years of any successful marriage is filled with the adjustments of expectations. Feelings get hurt; people are confused. They can use that situation as an opportunity to tell one another what they hoped would happen and how they felt when it didn't. Quite often, just bringing these expectations to the light of day works wonders for the couple's relationship.

There are unrealistic expectations in virtually every meaningful relationship simply because we are all fallen, imperfect people with holes in our lives. In Genesis we learn that a man and a woman "shall leave their father and mother and cleave to each other" (Genesis 2:24). The word *cleave* was used in that day to describe the gluing together of two pieces of papyrus to make one smooth writing surface. The holes in one were covered by the smooth places in the other. The two pieces need each other to be whole and smooth, and together they have much more value than when they were separate.

To facilitate open, honest communication, regularly ask open questions like: "I want to understand you. Would you please tell me more about. . . ?" As you enter the next level of communication, remember:

• Bite your tongue and listen.
• Ask second and third questions to be sure you understand.
• Accept any appropriate responsibility, but don't be a blame sponge.
• Don't gloss over real problems and pretend they aren't significant.
• Don't run away.
• Don't attack.

Good marriages (friendships, parent-child relationships, or business relationships) are not the union of perfect people. Good relationships are forged in the smelter of conflict and refinement. Climbing the ladder of intimacy is a glorious—but sometimes painful—process.

❏ How can you tell if someone is listening to you?

How can you tell if you are listening to others?

Who is the hardest person for you to listen to? Why? What can you do about it?

❑ Think of a time when someone genuinely affirmed you. Describe the situation and how you felt.

❏ List five people in your life. What do you appreciate about each of them? What is one specific thing you can do to affirm each one?

❏ List the people you have forgiven.

List those you haven't forgiven for betraying you, hurting you, ignoring you, or abandoning you.

Go back and read the paragraphs about forgiveness in this chapter. What are some benefits of forgiving people?

Forgiveness means choosing not to take revenge and instead wiping away a debt because our debt was wiped away by Christ's forgiveness. Does that encourage you to choose to forgive? Why or why not?

Are you ready to make that choice to forgive? Write out your statement of forgiveness of each person. Include the specific offense, how it hurt you, and your choice to forgive. Use additional paper if necessary.

❏ Is confronting people relatively easy or difficult for you? Explain:

❏ Is there someone you need to confront? If so, write out a plan based on the principles of confrontation in this chapter.

❏ What has given you the greatest joy in giving to others? Explain:

❑ Complete this inventory of you and your spouse or partner.

—Your personality type:

—Your spouse or partner's personality type:

—Describe characteristics of your normal communication.

—Describe characteristics of your stress/conflict communication.

—What "languages" do you speak and hear?

—What "languages" does your partner speak and hear?

—Expectations
What do you want/expect from your spouse or partner?

What does your spouse or partner want/expect from you?

Describe your expectations (realistic and unrealistic) with your spouse or partner concerning:

money—

sex—

children—

in-laws—

Where is your relationship on the ladder of intimacy? Draw a circle around the highest rung which represents your current relationship with your spouse or partner.

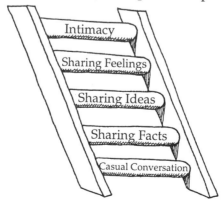

❏ Complete this inventory of you and your boss.
—Your personality type:
—Your boss' personality type:
—Describe characteristics of your normal communication.

—Describe characteristics of your stress/conflict communication.

—What "languages" do you speak and hear?

—What "languages" does your boss speak and hear?

—Expectations
What do you want/expect from your boss?

What does your boss want/expect from you?

Describe your expectations (realistic and unrealistic) with your boss concerning:

compensation—

performance—

relating to other employees—

office communication—

Where is your relationship on the ladder of intimacy? Draw a circle around the highest rung which represents your current relationship with your boss.

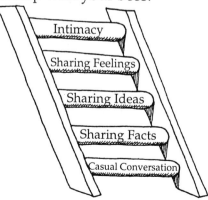

❏ Complete this inventory of you and your best friend.

—Your personality type:

—Your best friend's personality type:

—Describe characteristics of your normal communication.

—Describe characteristics of your stress/conflict communication.

—What "languages" do you speak and hear?

—What "languages" does your friend speak and hear?

—Expectations

What do you want/expect from your best friend?

What does your best friend want/expect from you?

Describe your expectations (realistic and unrealistic) with your best friend concerning:

time together—

depth of communication—

frequency of communication—

Where is your relationship on the ladder of intimacy? Draw a circle around the highest rung which represents your current relationship with your best friend.

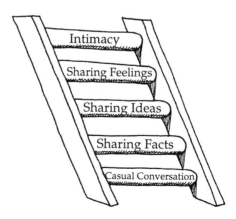

❑ Complete this inventory of you and your parents.
—Your personality type:
—Your mother's personality type:
—Your father's personality type:
—Describe characteristics of your normal communication.

—Describe characteristics of your stress/conflict communication.

—What "languages" do you speak and hear?

—What "language" does each of your parents speak and hear?
Your mother:

Your father:

—Expectations
What do you want/expect from your mother?

What do you want/expect from your father?

What does your mother want/expect from you?

What does your father want/expect from you?

Describe your expectations (realistic and unrealistic) with your parents concerning:

depth and frequency of communication—

your children—

their health needs—

financial needs—

Where are your relationships on the ladder of intimacy? Draw a circle around the highest rung which represents your current relationship with your mother and put an *M* next to it. Then draw a circle around the highest rung which represents your current relationship with your father and put an *F* next to it.

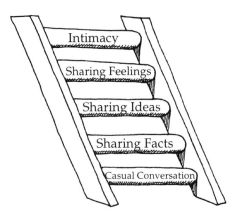

❏ Complete this inventory of you and your children.

—Your personality type:

—Your children's personality types:

—Describe characteristics of your normal communication

—Describe characteristics of your stress/conflict communication

—What "languages" do you speak and hear?

—What "languages" do each of your children speak and hear?

—Expectations
What do you want/expect from each of your children?

What do each of your children want/expect from you?

Describe your expectations (realistic and unrealistic) with your children concerning:

depth and frequency of communication—

privileges and responsibilities—

Where are your relationships on the ladder of intimacy? Draw a circle around the highest rung which represents your current relationship with each of your children and put their initials next to them.

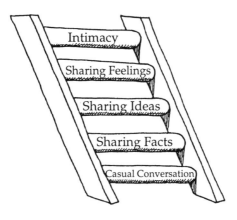

❏ Think of a friend, co-worker, sibling, or some other important person in your life. Complete this inventory of you and _____:

—Your personality type:

—_____'s personality type:

—Describe characteristics of your normal communication.

—Describe characteristics of your stress/conflict communication.

—What "languages" do you speak and hear?

—What "languages" does _____ speak and hear?

—Expectations
What do you want/expect from _____?

What does _____ want/expect from you?

Describe your expectations (realistic and unrealistic) with_____ concerning:

depth and frequency of communication—

time together—

Where is your relationship on the ladder of intimacy? Draw a circle around the highest rung which represents your current relationship with _____.

One Step at a Time

Trust takes time to build. Don't expect or demand that a rocky relationship make a dramatic U-turn and change completely overnight. The U-turn might occur instantaneously, but that is only the first step in a long process of growth and development. In many cases, years of trash and crud must be cleared away to allow room for hope and love. That clean-up campaign is just as much a part of the process as the more pleasant steps later on. It signifies an honest and sincere commitment to move forward no matter what the cost. But relationships always take two. You can't make another person love you, appreciate you, or value you. Take the steps you can take, and don't manipulate others to taking any steps. Let them be free to choose. If each person wants to make progress, wonderful things can happen in any relationship!

Make Changes Now

Thomas Carlyle was a Scottish essayist and poet who, late in life, married Lady Jane Welch. Not long after they were wed, they found out she had a chronic, terminal illness, possibly cancer. Carlyle was a famous man in his day. He traveled the world presenting his work to adoring crowds. When he was at home, he was often focused exclusively on his writing, and he sometimes didn't even see Lady Jane for days on end. The months passed, and eventually, Lady Jane died. She was buried in a country cemetery not far from Carlyle's home.

After the funeral, several friends went with Carlyle back to his house to be with him. He appreciated their friendship, but soon he needed to be alone. He excused himself and walked upstairs to Lady Jane's bedroom. Carlyle sat down in a chair next to her bed. After a few moments, he noticed a book on her nightstand. He picked it up. It was her diary. He began to read. Carlyle noticed that Lady Jane had put a star next to her entry on the days he came and sat with her. By the stars, she noted things like, "He came by today, and it was like heaven to me! I love him so." Carlyle continued reading. On the last day, when she was barely strong enough to write, there was no star in the diary. He read her words: "The day has grown long, and the shadows are up the hall. I've not heard his footsteps, and I know he'll not be coming today. Oh, how I wish I could tell him I love him so!"

Downstairs, Carlyle's friends were startled when he came tearing down the stairs and bolted out the door. One of them said, "The cemetery! Perhaps he's going to the cemetery." They ran to the graveyard where Lady Jane had been buried only hours earlier. A steady rain was falling now. When they arrived, they found Carlyle lying on the fresh dirt of his wife's grave. He was pounding his fist in the earth, saying over and over again, "If I had only known! If I had only known!"

I've heard it said many times that our last moments on earth will not be filled with regrets about unfinished goals, but with unshared love. Make a commitment to communicate your love often.

❏ Think of those most dear to you. If they died today, what would you wish you had done for them and said to them?

❏ What specific things can you do today to express your love for them?

10
Plotting Your Position

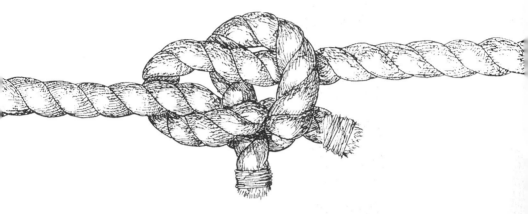

Dead reckoning is looking at the ship's log to determine where the ship has come from. Once that is learned, the navigator can accurately plot his position, analyze his resources, and chart his direction so he can stay on course in the future.

Looking at our present position (and condition) is probably encouraging in some ways . . . and painful in other ways. Most of us find our lives to be somewhat checkered as we do this exercise, but we can focus our attention soon on making the course corrections necessary to get where we want to go.

Author Robert Louis Stevenson said, "Sooner or later we all sit down to a banquet of consequences." We can make decisions about our choices, but we can't determine or orchestrate the consequences. We make our decisions, then our decisions make us.

❑ Describe your current status in relation to each of the North Star Principles. Identify your specific strengths and needs for each one.

—Embrace risk as a way of life.

—Take responsibility.

—Be honest about your emotions.

—Never stop learning.

—Value meaningful relationships.

—Develop spiritual strength.

—See life as an adventure!

❏ Make an inventory of where you are right now in each area of your life.

Describe the pros and cons of your current situation, and indicate your level of satisfaction in that area on a scale of 0 (The Titanic on the bottom) to 10 (The Titanic before it sailed).

What is true of me right now:

—My purpose in life
Pros:

Cons:

    0   1   2   3   4   5   6   7   8   9   10

—Marriage
Pros:

Cons:

    0   1   2   3   4   5   6   7   8   9   10

—Children
Pros:

Cons:

  0   1   2   3   4   5   6   7   8   9   10

—Career
Pros:

Cons:

  0   1   2   3   4   5   6   7   8   9   10
—Finances
Pros:

Cons:

  0   1   2   3   4   5   6   7   8   9   10

—Health

Pros:

Cons:

0   1   2   3   4   5   6   7   8   9   10

—Relationship with God
Pros:

Cons:

0   1   2   3   4   5   6   7   8   9   10
—Hobbies and leisure
Pros:

Cons:

0   1   2   3   4   5   6   7   8   9   10

—Lifestyle
Pros:

Cons:

0   1   2   3   4   5   6   7   8   9   10

—My sense of identity
Pros:

Cons:

0   1   2   3   4   5   6   7   8   9   10

❑ Now go back and put an arrow on each scale to indicate which direction you are going. (If you keep doing what you are doing, where will you be in a month, a year, or 10 years?) In which areas are you moving forward?

In which areas are you moving backward? Explain the reason:

Which area gives you the most hope? Explain:

Which area gives you the biggest red flag of concern? Why?

Motivations

A somewhat apocryphal story is told about Alabama football coach Bear Bryant who had a quarterback who was really slow. Alabama was winning a close Southeastern Conference game, and Bryant wanted his team to run out the clock. If they won, the Crimson Tide would move up in the polls the following week. It was (as all games are to Alabama fans) a very important game. Coach Bryant was shuttling tight ends to bring plays to the quarterback. The team on the field huddled. The tight end ran up and told the quarterback, "Coach Bryant said to run off tackle." The quarterback said, "No, that's what they expect us to do. We need some points to look better to the polls. We'll throw a pass." He told the split end to line up wide and go long. "I'll hit you down field." The tight end tried to protest, but the quarterback cut him short, "Hey, I'm the coach on the field, and we're going to throw a pass." He called the play and the team came up to the line of scrimmage. The split end walked a couple of steps wider than he had been before.

One of the defensive backs on the other side of the field noticed this split end was wide. He didn't move, but as soon as the ball was snapped, this back took off across and down the field. This guy was the 100 yard dash champ of the SEC. He could fly! The quarterback lofted a long pass to the wide open receiver. Like a blur, the defender came out of nowhere and intercepted the ball. He headed down the open sideline. The slim lead for Alabama was going to be wiped out in a few short seconds!

The quarterback took off after that defender. He caught him from behind on the 10 yard line as time expired on the game clock! The game was over. Alabama had won—barely.

On the other sideline, the coach for the other team just shook his head and laughed. When he met Coach Bryant in the middle of the field after the game, that coach smiled and said, "I thought you said that quarterback of yours is the slowest boy you'd ever coached. He just caught the fastest kid in the league from behind!"

Coach Bryant told him, "You've got to understand something, Coach. Your boy was running for six points. My boy was running for his life."

There are many motivations to encourage us to change: some are good, and some aren't so swift. If we change only to please a nagging spouse, boss, or child, we may be highly motivated to avoid that corrosive tongue, but any change will be half-hearted and probably temporary. I've watched a lot of people come to the point of change over the years. Here are some compelling reasons:

• Some people are fed up with their lives. They are bored. They have no purpose or passion, and they can't stand it anymore. They remember a time when life was fun and exciting, and they want to recapture that moment.

• They feel out of control. Life is too hectic. Too many people have too many demands on us, and we desperately need space, peace, and hope.

• Our anger is hurting others. We see its influence on our children, and we simply can't stand it. Our honest and painful conclusion is: "My kids are out of control because

I'm out of control. I just can't let that happen any longer." So we take whatever steps are necessary for the good of our children.

• Some of us have shouldered a heavy emotional burden so long that we are depressed. Clinical depression is when our bodies shut down and daily functions are impaired. When this happens, it is a wake-up call to get help.

• We experience a crises in our health, finances, marriage, or some other area of life. We realize that life has to change if we are to cope with the new situation.

• We need to simplify our lives. One of the trends of the past decade is for people in the corporate world to realize they are spending far too much time on money and acquisitions at the expense of those things that really matter—God and family. They realize these things make good servants but terrible masters.

• The consequences of the way we have been living is ruining our lives. Wrong choices have led to legal problems, financial missteps have led to bankruptcy, and addictive behaviors have led to severe medical problems.

In all these situations, there is one thing in common: We seldom change until we come to the end of our ropes. We have such a vested interest in maintaining the status quo that it takes a shock to jolt us into the commitment to make significant changes in our lives.

The greatest escape artist of all time, Harry Houdini, made a standing offer to any community that if he couldn't get out of their jail in a few minutes, he would pay them a sum of money. He had never failed in this challenge. One day, he went to a little community in Wales where he was locked in a cell. Seconds passed. Then minutes. Soon, the time was up, and Houdini was still in the cell. He had lost! All the people watching shouted. The jailer grabbed his keys to open the door, but Houdini snarled, "Don't touch that door! I'll work on it until I get out."

Some accounts say Houdini never escaped that cell. In the middle of the floor was a puddle of sweat where he had labored so hard to do what he had purposed to do. He dropped to his knees and in frustration pounded on the door. When he did, the jail door swung open. The jailor had forgotten to lock the door. The door was locked, however, in the most important place possible: Harry Houdini's mind.

Attitude makes all the difference in the world with how we handle opportunities and difficulties. I was traveling on Christmas Eve a few years ago. As I waited to check my luggage, I noticed the man in front of me being incredibly rude to the skycap. He was surly, demanding, and just downright mean. In fact, after the skycap finished with his luggage, the man didn't even tip him. The skycap never changed expressions. He whistled and smiled all the time. I walked up to him and said, "You've got a great attitude. I noticed that guy was rude to you, and he didn't even give you a tip."

The skycap smiled and winked at me. "Captain," he said to me, "that man is on his way to Los Angeles, but his bags are headed to Detroit." That just goes to show you: He who tags has the last laugh!

Sometimes people can really put us in our place. Years ago, Mohammed Ali was flying across the country. Before the plane took off, the stewardess came by and said, "You need to put on your seatbelt."

Ali looked at her and said, "Superman doesn't need a seatbelt."

Without a moment's hesitation, the stewardess shot back, "Superman doesn't need an airplane."

When we choose to change, those closest to us may object. They, like we, have become familiar and comfortable with the way things are—even if they are out of control.

Give yourself permission to change, and give those around you permission to struggle with how your changes affect them. Use this as an opportunity to communicate about important issues of expectations and hopes. All of you will need to be flexible to make this work, but this can be a time of genuine growth for everybody.

You Know It's Time to Change When . . .

Many of us avoid change until we are convinced the benefits far outweigh the risks of remaining stuck in the status quo. Here are some road signs that let you know your journey is at that point:

- Your sense of dissatisfaction can't be pinned down.
- You're tired of living below your potential.
- Your desire to change is *pushed up* by internal motivation, not *pumped up* by hype or *pulled out* by others.
- You may know where you've been, but you aren't sure where you're going.
- You start looking like the picture on your driver's license.
- You just know there's more to life than this!

❑ Look over the list of motivations in this chapter. Which ones motivate you to change? Explain:

❏ How will the changes you want to make potentially affect other people?

❏ How will you communicate clearly and help them understand the necessary steps of change?

Confucius, China's most famous teacher and philosopher, knew the importance of getting our hearts right as the foundation for all of our dreams, plans, and accomplishments. He said, "To put the world right in order, we must first put the nation in order; to put the nation in order, we must first put the family in order; to put the family in order, we must first cultivate our personal life; we must first set our hearts right."

❏ What does is mean to you to "first set your heart right"?

11
THE PROCESS OF CHANGE

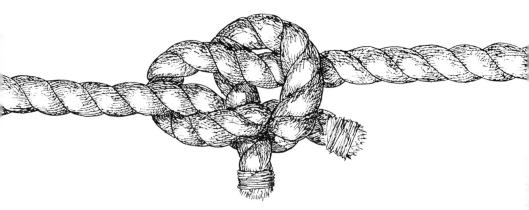

Peter Lynch was a Wall Street wizard. He built the Fidelity Magellan mutual fund to a $13 billion giant through shrewd investing and management. He was featured on scores of television programs targeted for investors. He was at the top of the mountain. Then one day, he quit. The 47-year-old Lynch realized his 14-hour workdays left little time for his family. He hardly knew his seven-year-old daughter. He walked away from Magellan so he could make his schedule fit his priorities. Investors in Magellan supported his move. Lynch received over a thousand letters of encouragement. He said, "I loved what I was doing, but I came to a conclusion, and so did some others: What in the hell are we doing this for? I don't know anyone who wished on his deathbed that he had spent more time at the office."

All across the country, people are reappraising their priorities and their careers. Boomers who thought the American dream was monetary wealth now realize their focus has been misplaced. Tens of thousands are leaving the rat race of corporate life to spend more time with their families and have more time for themselves. They will make less money, but that's a small price to pay for sanity.

The fuels for change are often like those used in a spacecraft. The first stages are powered by volatile, explosive liquid oxygen. In the same way, we are thrust into the process of change by the explosive motivations of fear, heartache, shame, and a longing for something more. Later stages of space flight are powered by thrusters which adjust the craft's attitude (its position in its line of flight). In the same way, our attitude is adjusted by a clear vision, thankfulness, and love as we continue on our journey.

Change is uncomfortable, but most of us simply won't take those necessary steps until and unless we feel uncomfortable enough. Ornithologists tell us that an eagle's nest, called an *aerie,* is an immense structure with new additions year after year. When the female eagle senses it is time for the eaglets to learn to fly, she "stirs the nest" by raking out the matted, soft, comfortable layer the eaglets have enjoyed since they broke out of their eggs. Now the nest is prickly and uncomfortable, so the young eagles move to the edge of the nest and flap their wings to strengthen them. When they take that first leap, some of them fly, but some fall like a rock. The mother eagle races under the falling young and carries it back to the nest to grow stronger and try again.

We may not leave the comfort of our nests until they become prickly. At that point, we begin to contemplate the possibilities of doing something different. Our first attempts my be successful, or they may be colossal failures. One of the important lessons we learn is that God allows us to keep trying until we learn to fly.

The more cautious among us usually attempt incremental changes, one small step at a time. If the status quo is deeply rooted, however, these small steps often fail to make much of a dent. Drastic action may be required. At this point, most of you Missouris and Paradise Stars are saying,

"See, I told you!" And you Intrepids and Calypsos are shaking in your boots! Hold on. It will make sense in a minute.

Some of us are so safety conscious that we think *any* change is drastic. Instead of embracing risk as a way of life, we embrace caution! I talked with a friend not long ago who was in the process of reshaping his career so he could have more time with his family. He is a cautious Calypso, and his first solutions were to work extra hours so he could make more money so his family could take a nicer vacation. That didn't achieve his goal of spending more time with his family. In fact, it was counterproductive. Then he decided to work two jobs and gradually move into the second one when it became more secure. He thought he could make enough money in 15 years to retire, but then he realized he would miss his kids' childhoods during that time. Ditto: It didn't work. Finally, some friends convinced him that he simply needed to make a job change, not work extra hours or two jobs. He screwed up the courage to make that choice, and he's been a much happier man ever since.

Other changes require more self-discipline, not drastic decisions. If the problem has been laziness, you need to get on a schedule. If the problem is overspending, you need a workable budget. In many cases, discovering your North Star includes both monumental choices and self-disciplined, incremental ones. Make sure your plan acknowledges the need for each.

Stages of Change

Most people who go through significant change in their lives and their careers can observe identifiable stages. Of course, we aren't robots who move from one gear to the next. Even if we don't follow these stages exactly, but they help us understand the ebb and flow of the process of change.

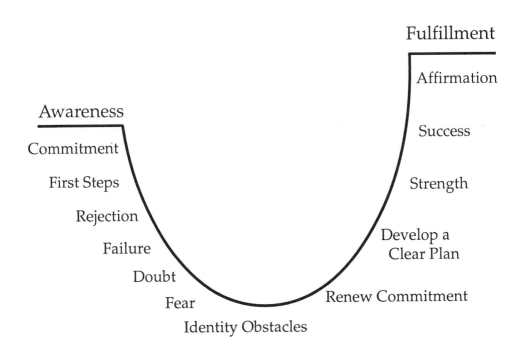

For the sake of clarity, we can identify six definite stages.

Stage 1—Awareness

In the last chapter, we looked at many motivations. Each of those begins with the awareness that (a) things aren't all that good, or (b) things could be a lot better. Maybe both. This may seem like an obvious place to start, but millions of people are mired in ruts because they don't open their eyes to see what is going on in their lives. The sooner we see, the sooner we can make changes.

Stage 2—First Steps

"Man, this is it! I finally have direction for my life!" I've heard people say that so many times, and I'm thrilled each time. People leave a seminar or finish a book, and they are ready to go! They get home and tell their spouse, "I've seen the light! We're making changes. Here's what we're doing. Pay attention." They walk through their office doors and proclaim, "From now on, things are going to be different around here!"

It takes about five seconds for a spouse to say, "Fat chance, Buck-o!" And not much longer for people at work to shrug, "I've heard that before. Let's go get a cup of coffee. He'll get over his crusade by the time we get back."

Quite often, they're right.

It is at this point that many of us fold our tents and quit. We've taken a shot at change, but people shot back! Initial enthusiasm rarely translates into lasting change. It requires much more stamina and wisdom to see it through.

Or we may rush out in great eagerness to change something, but we change the wrong thing. The results can be devastating. In its prime, the castle of the Castlereagh family was one of the finest in Ireland. Massive parapets and finely appointed staterooms made this a place of grandeur and beauty. Over the years, the need for protection from other feudal lords vanished. The castle became obsolete. Gradually, it fell into decay, and eventually the descendents moved away. Villagers used the cut stones of the castle to repair walls in their houses and to build roads. Slowly, the castle was being dismantled stone by stone.

Many years later, a family member, Lord Londonderry, visited the site and was aghast at the castle's condition. He was determined to end the stealing of stones from the castle, so he ordered a wall be built around its remnants. The wall was to be six feet tall, strong and stout to keep out those who would steal stones for their own use. He commissioned an overseer, and he left for England.

Several years later, Lord Londonderry returned to examine the castle. As his carriage turned the last bend, he peered around the corner to get his first glimpse . . . but the castle was gone! Entirely gone! As the carriage approached the scene, Lord Londonderry saw the wall enclosing the space where the castle had been. "But where is the castle?" he demanded.

"The castle, is it?" responded the caretaker. "I built the wall with it, my Lord. Is it for me to be going miles for materials with the finest stones in Ireland are beside me?"

Lord Londonderry had created change, but he had lost what was most valuable in the process.[1]

Stage 3—Regroup

So change isn't quite as easy as you hoped, huh? It's only a problem if you quit. But you won't. This is the time for honest reflection about the risks and rewards of going in a new direction and finding new meaning in life. I believe that this is the critical moment for most people. This is the real point of decision where the cost is counted, and the choice (based on hard realities and sound expectations, not pie-in-the sky easy dreams) is made to move ahead.

This is also the stage where the old tapes play loudest: "See, I told you that you'd never amount to anything! You're a failure! Nobody wants you!" The early setbacks set the stage for these tapes to play loudly and clearly, but we can replace them with new messages of hope and confidence. I know many men and women who memorize statements made by Zig Ziglar, Anthony Robbins, and other motivational speakers. I also recommend we replace old tapes with statements from the greatest motivational book of all time: the Bible. Paul wrote to the believers in Ephesus, saying:

> Now to Him who is able to do immeasurably more than all we ask or imagine, according to His power that is at work within us, to Him be glory in the church and in Christ Jesus throughout all generations. (Ephesians 3:20)

If we align our purpose with God's, He will pull out all the stops to do "immeasurably more than all we ask or imagine"! That's incredible, but that's exactly what it says. When the old tapes water the soil of doubt in our hearts, we can yank out those weeds and replace them with the strong healthy plants of faith that produce good fruit for us and those around us. Change may be difficult, but it provides us with wonderful opportunities to learn and grow. As my friend Ira Blumenthal says, "Change is inevitable. Growth is optional."

The regrouping stage is where we hone our new ways of thinking and measuring success. Things that used to seem so precious to us appear empty now. We measure success by the impact we have on others, not just the possessions and prestige we can acquire for ourselves. Our vision of the future is more expansive, because we are pursuing dreams that will make a difference in others' lives.

Make no mistake: There's a price we have to pay to reach our potential. We have to let go of one trapeze bar in order to grab another. We can't have both. As we regroup our thoughts in this stage, the benefits of focusing our lives becomes clearer and clearer. It's worth it, especially when we consider the cost of staying in the same rut—the frustration, the "what-if's," the "could-have-beens," and "would-have-beens."

Stage 4—Identify Obstacles

Benjamin Franklin is the source of the often-quoted statement, "Only two things are inevitable, death and taxes." But in our day, we might add another to that short list—change. We can choose some changes, but some are out of our control. For instance, we can choose whether to take a job in a different city, but we can't keep our children from growing up and moving out of our houses. We can't eliminate risks, but we can learn to manage them.

One of the most important things we can do is to identify the obstacles to change so we can take specific steps forward. We can live our lives by design or by default. Anticipating these obstacles lets us plan effectively so we don't get off track. Each of us needs to overcome these 12 hurdles:

1. The Law of Inertia.

The law of inertia states that an object at rest tends to stay at rest. Some of us simply refuse to take any steps of change at all. We have the privilege and the responsibility to choose many of the changes in our lives: where we work, who we marry, where we live, our friends, etc. Too often, we take the path of least resistance, hoping things will just work out. Actually, we abdicate many of these decisions and let others make them for us.

2. The Comfort Zone.

Some of us look at the changes that need to be made . . . then we look at the way things have been . . . and we conclude that it is much more comfortable to stay right where we are! Our main goal is not success and progress; it is avoiding change unless it is absolutely necessary. We fail to realize, however, that we pay a very high price for remaining stuck in the quagmire of mediocrity.

3. The Fear of Failing.

Some of us have very high standards for ourselves. Our

reluctance to change is not because we are comfortable where we are; the reluctance stems from the dread of trying and failing. Paradise Stars and Intrepids fear others' responses to their failure more than the actual failure itself.
4. Satisfaction.

Of course, some of us are simply happy with our lives and have no compelling motivation to change. Perhaps we have paid the price of change earlier in our lives and now reap the rewards. Change requires a strong commitment and a tenacity to wade through the situational mud that is always a part of making progress. Satisfied people don't have that commitment and tenacity.
5. Benefits and Liabilities.

If we aren't convinced that the benefits of the change outweigh the liabilities, we will fight change as long as we can...and that can be a very long time! Many of us love our routines and we want to stay in our comfort zones. It is often helpful to make a written, detailed list of benefits and liabilities, pros and cons, for an anticipated change. Seeing it in black and white often qualifies our nebulous fears and quiets the internal storm. On this list, we should include the risks and losses of not changing as well. This will give us added perspective.

There is always a price to be paid for any significant change. Some of this price is paid up front in the form of time for planning, explaining, and dreaming. Another price we pay is the stress we feel as we experience the fear of the unknown and the fear of failure. We also suffer when others don't understand or believe in our vision. That hurts. This is when many of us throw up our hands and quit because the price seems too high. But misunderstandings in the process of change are so common that we need to factor that in at the beginning! If we anticipate it, we won't be caught off guard and thrown off track. In the middle of the change, the price may be sleepless nights trying to figure out what steps to take next or the loss of friends if you have to move away. But here, too, if we have a clear vision and anticipate the price, we will be ready to meet those challenges.

6. A Lack of Effort.

Most changes require action. Even changes that are thrust upon us require action to respond properly. Many of us talk about taking action. We dream about what steps to take. We may even write out a plan, but some of us avoid taking those steps at all costs! On the other hand, some of us are compulsive doers. We jump to action without careful reflection and planning. Sometimes, the compulsive doers and the fearful non-doers are married to each other!

7. Refusing to Look at New Solutions.

The pace of change in today's Information Age is staggering. Almost every day we hear about a new software or a new computer technology that can do more, faster, and better than the day before. Some of us throw up our hands and say, "It's no use. I can't keep up." And some of us joke about being 19th century people on the brink of the 21st century. Yes, it's a challenge to keep up, but we need to pay attention to the new solutions to old problems or we'll be left behind.

8. Negativity.

Do you know people who can find something negative in even the most beneficial and pleasant change? I do. They gripe about anything and everything. To them, change necessarily means loss, so they resist any and all disruption in the way things are.

9. A Lack of Vision.

If we have a clear vision of where we want to go, we can take charge of our lives and make those decisions based on the consuming passion of our lives, not the whims of others. We don't need vision to make some changes happen, like death and taxes. But we need vision to know how to respond to them. When someone dies, a child grows up and moves away, or forced retirement rears its head, we need a clear sense that this, too, is a part of the unfolding of the plan for our lives. Our response to these negative changes can produce a deep, rich wisdom . . . or bitterness. It's all up to us.

10. A Lack of Confidence.

Battleships and cruise ships go places boldly, but sailboats and research ships are analytical, reflective, and often fearful. They can get stuck in "analysis paralysis" and think things to death without ever acting on them. Even those who seem the most confident on the outside may have deep, hidden fears that they might not be up to the task this time. If a person has experienced a particular change before, the level of confidence is directly related to that past experience. If a death in the family devastated the person years ago, he or she may anticipate the same heartache as another loved one nears death. These fears become self-fulfilling. Or if a job change has gone smoothly in the past and the person quickly developed good relationships with new co-workers, then he or she will have confidence in moving to a new job and relating to new people. That, too, becomes self-fulfilling.

11. Clinging to Tradition.

Traditions give stability to our lives. Families may go to the same places for vacations, or have the same breakfast on Christmas morning, or do the same special things on birthdays or anniversaries. There's nothing in the world wrong with reinforcing fond memories—unless these traditions get in the way of necessary changes. When patterns keep us stuck instead of providing appropriate stability, it's time to change those patterns. For example, one man insisted on protecting his tradition of coming home from work and reading the newspaper even when his young children clamored for his attention. That pattern of behavior had worked when he and his wife had no children, and he refused to change as his family situation changed. As you can imagine, his stubborn selfishness created tremendous tension in that home!

12. A Lack of Support.

We all need encouragement and feedback. We need the kindness and support of family and friends in the dreaming stage, the planning stage, and the action stage of change. A few of us are tough enough to force our way ahead without this encouragement, but we miss out on the wisdom a fellow traveler can give us along the way. Some of us won't take *any* steps without someone holding our hands. For these people, the changes are simply too threatening to even consider unless we feel the love (and maybe a gentle shove) of a close friend or family member.

You can be sure of death, taxes, and hurdles that need to be overcome. Anticipate them, expect them, and you will be more likely to eliminate or get around them.

Stage 5—A Clear Plan

Chapter 14 is devoted to the topic of planning, so we won't go into detail here. It is essential, however, that we prioritize and plan in order to succeed. Calypsos do this instinctively. So do most Intrepids and many Missouris. Paradise Stars on the other hand. . . .

Your plan is a wedding of your priorities, talents, and resources, and a realistic time frame. Too often we fail to marshall all these into a coherent plan of action. The plan may include some remedial steps to help you make the most progress possible. For example, if emotional baggage weighs you down, one of your priorities probably will be to address those untended wounds so you will be at peace.

Strained relationships may need attention. Perhaps they can be mended. If not, you can grieve the loss. Other health issues may be on the list, especially as people age beyond the middle adult years.

Some of the goals you set will be tangible and quantifiable, but some will have a qualitative nature, such as enriching your marriage. Even then, there are specific steps which can be taken to reach those unmeasurable goals.

Stage 6—Work the Plan

The long march in the right direction should be marked with many parties and celebrations for progress that has been made. Don't let the pursuit of your dreams turn into drudgery. Enjoy the journey as well as the destination. Sure, working the plan requires discipline and diligence to keep putting one foot in front of the other, day after day, but every day can be an adventure if we look for the good things and the good people around us.

When we work our plan, we aren't alone. When our dreams are in line with God's purposes, He makes things happen that one person described as "the surprise of the Spirit." Things fit together. People are encouraged. We see results where we've never seen them before. We have a sense of rightness about what we're doing. A strange and wonderful contentment sighs within us. We are partners with God.

We've all heard it said that good things come to those who wait. The Chinese bamboo tree is an amazing plant. In its first four years, the plant sees almost no growth at all. But the next year, it soars 80 feet tall! As we pursue our North Star, we will have to plow, hoe, weed, water, and wait before we enjoy the fruit of our efforts.

Sometimes we are disappointed with the lack of immediate results, but we must be patient. The growth will come.

And if we want to see truly remarkable results, we will need to work hard at preparation and planning. The higher we want to build a building, the deeper the foundation needs to be dug.

In 1976, Brett Butler was finishing high school. He dreamed of playing college baseball for Arizona State, one of the top college programs in the country. At the end of the season, Brett and his dad attended a sports banquet. After the dinner, the baseball coach got up and said something about each of the graduating seniors. When it came time for him to say something about Brett, the coach snickered, "Brett's goal is to be a major league baseball player, but he couldn't even start on our high school team!"

Brett was devastated. His dad leaned over and whispered, "Son, if you don't believe in yourself, nobody else will." Then his dad nodded and winked as if to say, "We'll show him!"

After realizing his dream to play at ASU, Brett was drafted in the 23rd round in the baseball draft and signed for the astronomical sum of $1000. But then he went to work in the batting cage, on his fielding, on his conditioning, and on every mental and physical aspect of the game. Hard work and persistence paid off. This tenacity and will to excel eventually made Brett into one of the greatest leadoff hitters baseball has ever known. One year, he got 42 bunt singles.

During spring training in 1996, Brett couldn't shake a sore throat. On May 2nd, he had a tonsillectomy. He thought his problems were over, but on May 5th, the doctors reported to him that he had cancer of the throat. On May 21st, he underwent radical cancer surgery.

Only a few months later, on September 6th, Brett returned to the field and was greeted by loud and long cheers from the many fans who love him. I wonder what his high school baseball coach would say now!

❑ Can you look back over your life and identify times when you made a fresh commitment to change and started with great enthusiasm but didn't get too far? Identify and describe some of those times here. (What commitments did you make? What steps did you take? What obstacles stopped you?)

❑ What are the specific issues you need to resolve in the regrouping stage, such as replacing old tapes with new messages, redefining success, and counting the cost? What difference will resolving these make?

❑ On a scale of 0 (not in the least) to 10 (like a brick wall), indicate the degree these obstacles blocked your progress. Explain your responses to those you score 1-3 or 8-10.

—The law of inertia   1   2   3   4   5   6   7   8   9   10

—The comfort zone   1   2   3   4   5   6   7   8   9   10

—The fear of failing   1   2   3   4   5   6   7   8   9   10

—Satisfaction   1   2   3   4   5   6   7   8   9   10

—Benefits and liabilities   1   2   3   4   5   6   7   8   9   10

—A lack of effort   1   2   3   4   5   6   7   8   9   10

—Refusing to look at new solutions

                    1 2 3 4 5 6 7 8 9 10

—Negativity   1 2 3 4 5 6 7 8 9 10

—A lack of vision   1 2 3 4 5 6 7 8 9 10

—A lack of confidence 1 2 3 4 5 6 7 8 9 10

—Clinging to tradition 1 2 3 4 5 6 7 8 9 10

—A lack of support   1 2 3 4 5 6 7 8 9 10

❏ Are you a good planner? Why or why not?

❏ What would help you plan more effectively?

❏ What are some rewards you can give yourself for making progress?

❑ Complete the following statements:
With my personality and background, the stage of change in which I do best is:

With my personality and background, the stage where I have the most difficulty is:

To make better progress, I need:

12
ASSISTANCE AND ACCOUNTABILITY

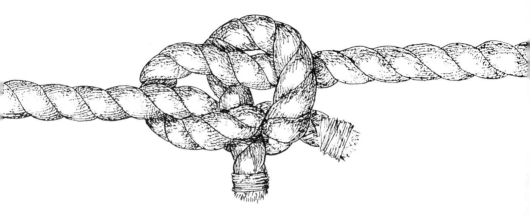

The pressures of life can be overwhelming. We can easily and quickly feel out of control, and when we feel that way, our behavior may get out of control as well. People who are angry or withdrawn often don't have anyone who cares about them . . . or they haven't revealed enough about their pain to give others the opportunity to show they care.

A man who had three sons—the middle one, a fifth grader, was mentally slow—heard all three boys fighting in the back yard. He went out to calm them down. He quickly learned that his slow son had started the fight with his seventh-grade brother. The second grader quickly jumped in, and it became an all-out war! The dad got them to stop. They were all in a circle, the boys were breathing heavy and glaring at each other.

"What happened?" the dad asked.

The youngest pointed to the slow brother and said, "He started it!"

The oldest boy nodded toward his brother, "He started it, Dad."

The middle son's head drooped to his chest. "Son, why did you start a fight with your brothers? What did they do to you?"

The boy looked up at his dad. A tear slid down his cheek. He stammered, "There's this boy at school. He makes fun of me. He waits outside the door when we go to lunch. He makes fun of the way I talk and all. He calls me 'stupid,' and tells me I'm dumb."

Now three others had tears on their cheeks. The oldest son put his hand on his brother's shoulder and asked a three word question: "What's his name?"

There was something about the tone in the oldest brother's voice that let his wounded brother know, "Don't worry about that bully. I'll take care of him for you."

Sometimes we keep our hurts bottled up. If we open up, we just might find a big brother or sister who cares.

Loneliness is a killer. It destroys motivation and confidence. We all need someone to believe in us and keep us going in the right direction. Recently, I was in Talahassee, Florida, in the weight room at Florida State University with Clint Purvis, chaplain of the football team, and Andre Wadsworth, who was a first round draft pick of the Arizona Cardinals (the third pick overall). Clint told me about the day five years ago when he first met with Andre. Andre was a walk-on as a freshman. He had high hopes of making the team, and he worked really hard to get ready to compete. At the end of the season his freshman year, he was still on the scout team, seemingly going nowhere fast. At the Orange Bowl in Miami, Florida, Clint saw Andre come off the practice field. His head was down. His shoulders slumped. Clint asked Andre, "What's wrong? Do you want to talk?" Andre shrugged and nodded.

Andre told Clint that he didn't know if college football was for him. He was really discouraged. Clint listened carefully and patiently, then he asked Andre if he could pray for him. The two men prayed together, and when Clint said "Amen," he turned to Andre and told him, "You can't quit. You're going to become a starter. In fact, you're going to be an All American. You're going to win the Lombardi Trophy for the top lineman in the nation, and after that, you're going to be a first round draft pick in the NFL!"

As I sat in that weight room with these two men, I realized, that's almost exactly what happened! The only thing that didn't work out as Clint predicted was that Andre came in second in the Lombardi voting. Clint shook his head and smiled, "I don't know why in the world I said all that to Andre. I guess God showed me something in him that he didn't see."

Indeed. That's what a mentor and encourager does for people. And it makes all the difference in the world! Embracing risk, taking responsibility, being honest, always growing, learning to trust the right people, developing spiritual strength, and seeing life as an adventure all require a supportive partner if we are to achieve our potential in life. We can try it on our own, but driving for success by ourselves leaves us empty and angry. We need the encouragement—and sometimes we need the correction—of people who care enough to tell us the truth.

But we don't always get encouragement from those we hope will give it. Bishop Milton Wright was a noted churchman who lived around the turn of the century. He often spoke at large conferences. At one of these, a man in the audience asked him, "Bishop Wright, do you think men are meant to fly?"

The bishop replied sharply, "Only angels are meant to fly. Not men."

The man's question had pertinence because dozens of people in Europe and in the United States were racing to be the first to create a heavier-than-air flying craft. At the time that question was asked, two brothers named Orville and Wilbur were on the dunes at Kitty Hawk, North Carolina, attempting to get their winged contraption off the ground. After painstakingly refining their measurements and redesigning their craft, they were the first ones to accomplish manned flight in a motorized airplane. They flew! And by the way, these brothers were the sons of one who didn't believe in their dream—Bishop Milton Wright.

People live for encouragement, and they die without it. All of us, even the most battle-hardened Missouris, need affirmation and encouragement. Positive messages are a cool drink of water on a hot, dusty day. But we need that encouragement from someone who is honest and perceptive. Most of us can't stand fluff! We want the truth, but we'd rather hear the encouraging part of that truth first!

Some of us balk at being held accountable for our decisions. I know men and women who have felt blasted in the past by parents or bosses, and they wince every time somebody asks them about a deadline or the progress of a project. Some of these folks already are driven obsessively to get things done, so they don't see the need to have somebody else "breathing down their necks." Others are not obsessive. They're lazy. They, too, don't want anybody asking questions and giving deadlines because it reminds them of their failure to get things done. Accountability can be administered harshly, but it can also be one of the most loving, positive, encouraging parts of a mentoring relationship. Trust is the key. If we trust the person holding us accountable—and if that trust is rewarded with the mentor graciously moving us along in our own way, at our own pace, sometimes pushing a bit, sometimes slowing us down—then accountability is not a pejorative. It is a blessing.

We also need someone who cares enough to speak the truth to us in love. When we are going in a particular direction, we are much more likely to listen to a positive, affirming person who says, "Wait. I think you might be getting off track." We tend to tune out the constantly negative people, or worse, we might be determined to prove them wrong and plunge ahead! The person who provides assistance and accountability might be your spouse, a close friend, a pastor, a counselor, or a paid consultant. Here is a checklist of characteristics to look for:

• A person whose life is one you want to emulate.
• A proven track record of perception and honesty.
• A person who understands and appreciates your gifts and abilities, and who understands your weaknesses.
• An open-minded person who can see new opportunities.
• An analytical, observant person who notices nuances of design and motivation.
• An honest person who will give corrective as well as affirming feedback.
• A person who is available.
• A person with some knowledge about the area of your interest.
• A person who can provide other resources to help you.
• A person who will hold you accountable to make progress in your commitments.

Perhaps no one fits all of these criteria, but look for someone who fits best for you. Some of the most available people may be convenient, but they may also lack some of the other essential criteria. Keep looking until you find someone who can provide the input you need. Don't try to go it alone!

On our own we are short-sighted with tunnel vision. We may see parts of the picture with crystal clarity, but we will miss other important parts. God has made us relational people. We need each other. Relationships are not a luxury; they are a necessity. Without relationships, some of us quit too soon; others become obsessed with achievement and acquisition, or become perfectionistic and narrow.

I also recommend you consider some dead people to be your mentors. That's right. Dead people. Some of the most inspiring people to me are those I have read about in biographies and histories. Their vision, tenacity, heart, and ability to overcome incredible odds always encourages me to keep going. Read about them. It will inspire you, too.

Tapes are another way to gain insight from others. Riding in my car or working at home, I have been privileged to listen to some of the greatest minds in America. These men and women ride along with me or sit next to me at home and share the secrets they have learned over a lifetime of struggle and success. What a privilege to have them nearby!

Some of us have great difficulty trusting others with our heart's desires. Perhaps we have been burned too many times in the past. We feel betrayed and hurt, and it seems safer to maintain arms-length relationships with others. Missouris and Calypsos have this tendency to go it alone if they've been hurt deeply in the past. Paradise Stars and Intrepids may isolate themselves, but they have a deep, compelling longing for trustworthy relationships.

Don't give up hope. Don't crawl into a cocoon to isolate yourself. No matter how deep your hurt or bitter the betrayal, you can find someone to trust again. Keep looking.

Diane Pearce, a professional counselor, told me a story of ten children whose parents were mentally ill and unable to care for them. The authorities had to split up the children because they couldn't find anyone to take all of them. The oldest child, a girl, was adopted at the age of five. The adoptive parents grew to resent this girl due to their marital problems. The situation was tolerable for a while, but as the girl entered puberty and began to develop physically, the mother determined to make this girl as unattractive as possible to boys in town. She refused to allow her to bathe. The girl had head lice, and she was forced to wear the same clothes day after day. The mother tried to keep the girl from going to school, but the truant officers forced her to allow the girl to attend high school. It was a mixed blessing. The girl's nickname at school was "Dog" because the adoptive family had almost 100 dogs—living *inside* the house. Dog feces stuck to her shoes, and the smell permeated her already-filthy clothes.

This girl sat in the stairwell of the bus to get away from the other children. She often thought of how she could fall out and let the bus run over her. That would end her pain. Day after day, week after week, this lonely, abused girl suffered at home and at school.

One day two girls in her class walked up to her. One of them said, "I want you to know that God loves you." Before she could say anything, the girl continued and asked, "Would you like to go to church with us this Sunday?" The girl nodded awkwardly. For the first time, they saw her smile.

The girl was so excited! She went home that day and burst through the door to tell her adoptive mother the good news. But when she said she had been invited to church, her mother growled, "No. I forbid it. You can't go." From time to time the girl slipped away from home on Sundays to go to meet those this girl at her church. There she heard more about a God who loved her.

The situation at her home was so tense, so abusive, that the girl ran away one day and went to Child Protective Services to tell them what was going on. The official said, "We had heard about your parents, and have been investigating. You don't have to go back. In fact, you don't ever have to go back there." CPS called the parents of another girl who had invited her to church to ask if she could spend the night with their family. They agreed, and one night turned into two, then a week, a month, and finally, permanent residence.

The new family loved her and patiently taught her to be a lady. She learned the basics of hygiene and manners, and she learned to love and be loved. After she graduated from high school, this girl went to college, earned her degree, and then went to graduate school to get her master's degree in counseling.

At that point in her story, Diane looked at me and said softly, "Ike, I'm Dog." I was shocked. It was astounding to think of this refined, gracious, lovely woman as a misfit child smelling like dog feces and unable to relate to people. She told me, "The day someone took the initiative to love me, my life changed. That love made all the difference in the world."

❏ Think of an instance or two when someone deeply encouraged and affirmed you. Describe the event(s), what the person did or said, and your response.

❏ Who are some people who have been mentors to you in the past? What difference did they make in your life during those times?

❏ Is accountability attractive to you? Why or why not?

❏ Do you have a mentor now? Do you want one? Why or why not?

❑ Look at the list of criteria for mentors. Rate the importance of each one these on a scale of 0 (thanks, but no thanks) to 10 (gotta have it):

___A person whose life is one you want to emulate.

___A proven track record of perception and honesty.

___A person who understands and appreciates your gifts and abilities, and who understands your weaknesses.

___An open-minded person who can see new opportunities.

___An analytical, observant person who notices nuances of design and motivation.

___An honest person who will give corrective as well as affirming feedback.

___A person who is available.

___A person with some knowledge about the area of your interest.

___A person who can provide other resources to help you.

___A person who will hold you accountable to make progress in your commitments.

❑ Write a summary statement.
  I need a mentor who will . . .

13
GETTING INTO THE GULF STREAM

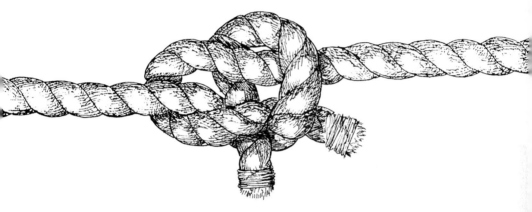

A friend of mine loves to go fishing offshore. He has gone off the coast of North Carolina several times to fish for marlin, tuna, and dolphin (the fish, not Flipper!). He departs from the beautiful little town of Beaufort and heads east past Cape Lookout and then past Cape Hatteras. About 40 miles from Beaufort, the water changes color. It is several degrees warmer, and there are far more fish in the water. The water color turns from green to blue at the edge of the Gulf Stream, a huge river of ocean water beginning in the Caribbean and flowing northeast to Iceland and Britain.

In that blue water, life is more abundant. Fishermen know they will catch far more if they fish in the Gulf Stream, so they make sure they go the extra distance to get there. It's the same for us. God's presence and power are the Gulf Stream of the human spirit. There, life is far more abundant, more rich and real. A fisherman can do exactly the same things in the green water as he does in the blue, but the results won't be the same. You and I can do the same things apart from God's presence and power, but it just won't be the same. The spiritual dimension makes a tremendous difference in every single facet of our lives. We need to do whatever it takes to find the Gulf Stream of God's Spirit and stay in that warm, abundant current so our lives will be richer and more rewarding.

Most of us are very familiar with Jesus' Sermon on the Mount where He gave the Beatitudes to His disciples. Each of His statements begins, "Blessed are those...." The word *blessed* means a self-fulfilling contentment. The island of Cyprus is called "The Blessed Isle" because it had everything it needed for the people to live healthy, happy lives.

When you and I are humble, honest about pain, gentle, hungering for what is right, merciful, pure in heart, eager to make peace, and willing to be criticized for doing right (those are character qualities listed in the Beatitudes), then we are probably experiencing self-fulfilling contentment. We aren't swayed by others' demands and whims. We are strong enough to be gentle and kind, wise enough to value the right things, and gracious enough to pursue peace in difficult circumstances. These are not just pious philosophical goals. They are the deep work of God's Spirit. They cannot be accomplished apart from God producing them in our hearts.

What does it mean to be in the Gulf Stream of God's Spirit? It means we experience His presence, wisdom, power, and pardon. It also means that we have meaningful relationships with His people. Let's look at each of these.

God's Presence

The prophet Elijah looked for God in the tornado, but He wasn't there. He found God when he was quiet enough to hear a "still, small voice." It is difficult for us to experience the presence of God in the whirlwind of activity in our lives. We need to get away so we can really listen to Him. In those times, He lets us know His purpose. We draw on His strength. Experiencing His presence gives us peace in the midst of the storm of stress and activity, or in the midst of opportunities and fun. As we develop our awareness of God in silence and solitude, we will learn to be more aware of Him in normal daily life, too. In the old classic, *Practicing the Presence of God*, Brother Andrew talked of experiencing God's wonderful presence in the most mundane human activities, such as washing dishes, changing diapers, and talking to friends. That awareness doesn't come easily. It must be cultivated over time.

Some people see God as a crutch. I see Him as an incredibly strong, loving person who reaches out and touches people like you and me. Sometimes I think about the Gospel accounts of Jesus touching people. He didn't just preach to them, though His words were the highest and purest ever heard. He didn't just do miracles, though His power is far above any other in the universe. He reached out and touched people: the blind man, the beggar, the lame, the children, the women, the tax gatherers, the lepers, the disciples.

A man recently asked me, "Ike, when you became a believer, did you believe there was a God, or did you *want* to believe there was a God?" That's a very good question. I thought for a moment and told him, "Initially I wanted to believe, but once I experienced Him, I knew."

We experience God's presence as we respond to His love and line up our lives with His purposes. Jesus told His disciples, "Whoever has My commands and obeys them, he is the one who loves Me. He who loves Me will be loved by My Father, and I too will love him and show Myself to him" (John 14:21). Isn't that what we want? To experience the loving presence of God? Jesus promised He would make Himself real to us as we follow Him.

Years ago, I went through the darkest, deepest valley of my life when my wife, Cindy, and our baby died in childbirth. For weeks after that tragic day, I wasn't sure I wanted to live. The oppression of the loss of my family was overwhelming. One day, I went to the jeweler to pick up a ring which had been made from a snowflake necklace that I had given Cindy. On the way home, my emotions overwhelmed me. I pulled over on the side of the road and wanted to die. At that moment, God spoke very warmly and clearly to me. He gave me a promise that He would fill the hole in my aching heart. It was very specific. It was unmistakable. I have felt God's presence on many occasions but probably no other time that I was at such a point of great need. That was a wonderful—and welcome—gift to me.

God's Wisdom

Knowledge is the accumulation of facts; wisdom is knowing how to use them. In today's technological revolution, we have a profusion of knowledge. Every person with a computer has the world at his or her fingertips through the Internet. Television news takes us around the globe for breaking events as they occur. The body of knowledge in the world is increasing at a phenomenal rate, perhaps doubling every few years, yet people are no wiser. James, the half-brother of Jesus, wrote, "If any of you lacks wisdom, he should ask God, who gives generously to all without finding fault, and it will be given to him" (James 1:5). But James includes a condition: "But when he asks, he must believe and not doubt, because he who doubts is like a wave of the sea, blown and tossed by the wind" (James 1:6). I like knowing I have a Friend who is a lot smarter than me!

James goes on to contrast the wisdom that we usually pass off as brilliance, and the wisdom of God:

> Who is wise and understanding among you? Let him show it by his good life, by deeds done in the humility that comes from wisdom. But if you harbor bitter envy and selfish ambition in your hearts, do not boast about it or deny the truth. Such "wisdom" does not come down from heaven but is earthly unspiritual, of the devil. For where you have envy and selfish ambition, there you find disorder and every evil practice.
>
> But the wisdom that comes from heaven is first of all pure; then peace-loving, considerate, submissive, full of mercy and good fruit, impartial and sincere. Peacemakers who sow in peace raise a harvest of righteousness. (James 3:13-18)

The centerpiece of wisdom is not accomplishment. James makes that very clear. The heart of wisdom is how we treat people. It is filled with honesty, integrity, forgiveness, kindness, and grace. In this we follow the example of Jesus. He saw people for who they could be, not just who they had been. He accepted them. Even the lepers, prostitutes, and tax gatherers felt the warmth of His love. And His love always found practical expression. He washed feet, fed the hungry, and encouraged the fainthearted. Jesus touched the lives of many people. His relationships were "up close and personal." He didn't just tell people what to do from an ivory tower.

In our day, many people have a vending machine concept of God. We put in our coins of doing something right or praying, and we're supposed to get whatever we want. God is far more concerned with our character than He is with our comfort. Transitions are often very difficult because our stability is shaken. We feel lost...out of control, but we can feel that way and be right in the center of God's will.

First Kings 17 tells how the prophet Elijah was sent by God to Kerith Ravine, east of the Jordan River. The word *Kerith* means "the cutting place." While Elijah was there, God did some cutting on Elijah's life. When Elijah arrived at Kerith Ravine, God sent ravens to bring him food. The creek in the ravine provided water. We sometimes make this scene look like a fairy tale, but the food the ravens brought was probably from a garbage dump, not the drive-thru and McDonalds! The creek and the ravens provided for Elijah for a while, then the creek dried up. Was Elijah where God wanted him? Absolutely. Were things going well? Absolutely not.

The passage states, "Then the word of the Lord came to him: 'Go at once to Zarephath of Sidon and stay there. I have commanded a widow in that place to supply you with food' " (I Kings 17:8-9). How long was Elijah without water before God sent him to the widow? We don't know. It may have been an hour, a day, a week, or a month. And how was Elijah feeling during that time? I don't know, but *I'd* have been wondering what was going on! Did God forget me? Did I do something wrong to deserve this? Elijah stayed where he was until God's word came to him clearly. And where did he go? To Zarephath, which means *refining*. God wasn't through with Elijah's course on character building!

I had become very secure in my career in Fayetteville, but I felt it was time to leave there and do something new. A door opened for me to take a wonderful position in Atlanta, but in my new role there, the creek dried up. For the first time in my adult life, I failed. For the first time, I hit a wall in a relationship. I simply couldn't love and encourage people enough to make it work. I took a risk to speak some hard truth to them, but they couldn't handle it. The tension was palpable. I knew it was time to leave . . . even if I had nowhere to go.

When I left New Hope Church in Fayetteville, I felt like Elijah. God was clearly leading me to go somewhere I hadn't planned to go, and when I got there, the creek dried up! I stayed and waited . . . and waited . . . and waited. During that time I thought about my priorities and values. I reflected on my goals in life and my motivations. I doubt if I would have thought as deeply if the creek of success hadn't dried up for a while. I waited there until I got a clear word from God to leave. At that point, I knew I was leaving, but I had nowhere to go! I knew I had to hear from God, so I got alone with Him and listened for several days. It was in that rich, deep experience that I heard from Him. It was a difficult process—one I would never have chosen—but one that has been well worth it.

We have so many distractions today that it is very difficult to listen to God. The prophet Jeremiah quoted God, " 'Then you will call upon Me and come and pray to Me, and I will listen to you. You will seek Me and find Me when you seek Me with all your heart. I will be found by you,' declares the Lord" (Jeremiah 29:12-13). Listening to the Lord is not a casual, easy thing like turning on the radio in the car on the way home. It requires us to search with all our hearts, with intensity and tenacity. Pursuing Him can be a draining experience, as well as an encouraging one. Searching for the wisdom of God is like mining for gold. It requires effort, attention, and time, but it can be one of the most rewarding experiences of our lives. I wanted to be alone with God, so I went back up to the mountains of North Carolina to where I grew up. I had no television or radio. There were no distractions, only time and silence. I also spent a few days at a cabin in north Georgia. That was where God impressed me to read about Abraham in Genesis. Abraham was alone and without direction, and God told him to go outside and look at the stars. God told him his descendents would be as numerous as the stars in the sky. I walked outside and looked at the night sky, and I saw the North Star. At that moment, I knew God was speaking to me, too. The North Star has always been the point of reference for travelers. I knew it was time to start a church that provides a point of reference for people in their journey.

I believe all God-given dreams have three parts: birth, death, and rebirth. After my stream had dried up and my dream died, God gave it a rebirth in what I'm doing now. My North Star is to build, encourage, and challenge men and women to achieve their potential. The rebirth of that dream has involved great risks. We began our church with no budget, but we began with some wonderful people. Over time, the unfolding of that dream has been more fulfilling than anything I can imagine. My experiences of the past couple of years has renewed my faith in a miracle-working God, whose eyes are not so dim that He cannot see my problems, His ears are not so dull that He doesn't hear my prayers, and His arms are not too short to reach into my predicament and divinely intervene. He is God, and He still moves the stones of disappointment that try to keep me in the grave of doubt.

God's Power

I'm not just a chemical reaction of natural determinism. Our universe is an open system, not a closed one that operates on its own. It is open to the hand of God creating and sustaining life, planets, and purpose. The power of God is awesome, but it is not a magic wand for us to use in any way we choose. He reserves His power for those who are intent on honoring Him with the results. God won't unleash His power in the lives of people who aren't in tune with Him and His purposes. But when we are, He will move heaven and earth to accomplish His purposes through us.

Sometimes God's power works in incredible ways. When I was in college, I worked as a janitor and a youth minister at a church to try to make ends meet. My tuition was due, but I didn't have the money. I pulled out of my driveway one morning. I usually turned to the left, but for some reason I felt strongly that I should go the other way. I turned right and drove through the neighborhood. When I drove by a little church, the pastor, Herb Wilson, was raking the front yard. He saw me and waved to me. I pulled over and got out of the car. He said, "You won't believe this, but I was just thinking about you. The fellow who was supposed to speak at our church this week got sick, and I want you to fill in for him. Will you do it?"

For some reason, I said "Yes." That first night I preached every sermon I had in my files. I have no idea what I said the rest of the week. At the end of the week, the church took up an offering for me. When they counted the money, it came to exactly the amount I owed the school for my tuition. God had orchestrated every detail, even leading me to turn right instead of left that morning.

Another way God worked powerfully in my life was when I applied to Mercer University. One little problem: They turned me down . . . twice. When I got the news the second time, I was really down. As I walked away from the campus, a woman stopped me and asked, "Are you OK?"

I said to her, "No, not really."

She probed, "What's wrong?"

"I wanted to go to school here. I believe this is the place where I'm supposed to get my education. In fact, I left my job so I could go here, but I've been rejected twice."

She looked surprised. "Come with me," she said as she started walking toward the admissions office.

When we entered the building, she led me through a door that said Dean on it. I assumed she was the dean's secretary or a good friend of the dean. I was wrong. She *was* the dean! She leaned back in her chair and told me, "Ike Reighard, if you really mean what you say about your commitment to work hard and do well here at Mercer, I'll allow you in on a probationary status."

"Really? That's great!" Probation sounded like heaven to me!

I graduated magna cum laude from a four-year program in two-and-a-half years. (I would have settled for "laudy have mercy," but magna cum laude looked really good on that diploma!)

Is this an example of God's power? You bet! God had me walk past that dean at just the time she would see me and be receptive. And the experience of getting in "by the skin of my teeth" probably had something to do with my desire to excel in school. The fingerprints of God's power and mercy were all over that experience! Timing is the essence of a miracle, and this was an example of God's perfect timing!

God's Pardon

The two best feelings in the world are being forgiven and forgiving others. Some of us have done some pretty bad things. We've hurt people. We've cursed God. We may feel we've crossed the line and we can never be forgiven. We live under a dark cloud of guilt. We laugh, and we have friends, but we can't escape that cloud. Here's great news: There's nothing so bad, nothing so evil, nothing so secret that God can't forgive.

I often think of David. He loved God, and he was a true hero. He became king of Israel, and God made a covenant with him so that his descendents would sit on the throne of Israel forever. David had it made! He was a songwriter and a skilled musician. He was a gifted athlete, and as a politician, David united a divided country. But he had a character flaw of enormous proportions.

One day his army troops were off fighting a war while he stayed behind in Jerusalem. He walked out on his balcony to stretch his legs, and he saw a beautiful woman taking a bath on the roof of a nearby house. Her name was Bathsheba. She was the wife of Uriah, one of David's soldiers at the battle. David knew he should turn around and walk back inside, but he didn't. He asked about the woman and was told she was the wife of Uriah the Hittite. He had the woman brought to him. He could have stopped there, too, but he didn't. He had sex with her and sent her home. David abused his God-given role as the leader of his people.

After a few weeks, she sent word back that she was pregnant. David had a solution. He sent for Uriah to come back from the battle. When Uriah arrived in Jerusalem, David asked him for news from the battle and then told him to go to his house so he could have sex with his wife. Then, David surmised, Uriah would think the child was his own. But Uriah was too honorable. He refused the privilege because his fellow soldiers couldn't enjoy the same privilege with *their* wives. David tried again. He got Uriah drunk and told him to go home. Again, Uriah refused to go home and be alone with Bathsheba.

David now went to Plan C. He sent a message to the commander of the army (in fact, he put the sealed paper in Uriah's hand to carry) and told the commander to put Uriah in the front of the battle and then withdraw from him so he would be killed. The commander did exactly that, and Uriah was riddled with arrows.

It was over. The secret was safe.

Or was it? God knew, and He made sure that David remembered his sins of adultery and murder. Finally, the combination of guilt and the confrontation by the prophet Nathan caused David to confess his sin and accept God's forgiveness. David described his guilt and confession in Psalm 32:3-5:

> When I kept silent,
>> my bones wasted away
>> through my groaning all day long.
> For day and night
>> your hand was heavy upon me;
> my strength was sapped
>> as in the heat of summer.
> Then I acknowledged my sin to you
>> and did not cover up my iniquity.
> I said, "I will confess
>> my transgressions to the Lord"—
> and you forgave
>> the guilt of my sin.

Sin always takes us further than we thought we would go. It keeps us longer than we ever thought we would stay. And it makes us pay more than we ever would have been willing to pay. David experienced severe consequences for his sins, but God forgave him and did not make him pay the ultimate price for his sins—death.

If God forgave David for adultery and murder, surely he will forgive you and me. We can be sure of it. Many of us think we need to pay for our own sins by feeling bad enough long enough. But how bad do we need to feel? And how long do we need to feel that way? We have accurately perceived that sin is serious business. That is true. But a very serious price has been paid for our sins: the death of the sinless Messiah, God's own Son. His death is the payment for every sin ever committed. His last words on the cross were "Paid in full."

Paul gives us a powerful illustration of forgiveness in his letter to the Colossians. He compares guilt to a debtors' prison where a list of debts was posted on the door until they were paid off. Speaking of Christ, Paul wrote, "He forgave us all our sins, having canceled the written code, with its regulations, that was against us and that stood opposed to us; He took it away, nailing it to the cross" (Colossians 2:13b-14). That code, or list of debts, was against us because it kept us in prison. Jesus took that list from our prison door and nailed it to His prison door, the cross, where He paid for it in full.

We don't have to beg God to forgive us. He has already done it. We need to gratefully and humbly accept His incredible gift of forgiveness and then live in a way that honors the One who died for us. Will we feel different when we accept God's forgiveness? Probably, but maybe not. Some of us are so consumed with guilt that we must begin with an act of the will to accept God's forgiveness. Only later will we feel what we have experienced. Corrie ten Boom used to say, "God buries our sin in the deep blue sea. Then He puts up a sign that says, 'No fishing.' "

God has given us a wonderful opportunity to clean up the past as a foundation for the future. If we have wounded others, we can go to them to confess our sins against them. If we have taken anything, we can restore it and make it right. The law of the land may not require that we make restitution, but the law of God and the law of the heart require that we take any steps necessary to pay back what we have stolen or broken.

Bask in the incredible forgiveness of God. As you understand its depth and breadth, you will learn to relax and enjoy God's wonderful love.

God's People

In the years that I have followed Christ, I have been comforted, encouraged, befriended, and challenged to excel by scores of wonderful brothers and sisters in the faith. Many of my best memories are of these dear friends who have loved me over the years, and some of my best laughs have been because of some of these people, too! But some of us haven't felt as encouraged as I have.

Jeff VanVonderen wrote a book called *When God's People Let You Down*. Some of us feel we could have been co-authors with Jeff. We feel deeply disappointed. We trusted in some believers. We hoped they would be kind and gracious to us, but they let us down. Perhaps our expectations were far too high. Or perhaps we were naive and didn't notice the warning signs. Either way, we feel deeply betrayed.

If that is your story, please don't give up. I know there can be Christian buzzards, but I also know some of God's choice men and women who are as loving and trustworthy as any human being can be. These people are reflections of the goodness and the strength of God as they encourage other people. They exemplify the fruit of the Spirit Paul mentioned to the Galatians: "But the fruit of the Spirit is love, joy, peace, patience, kindness, faithfulness, gentleness, and self-control" (Galatians 5:22-23).

And of course, most believers are somewhere in between. We all have our warts. We all let people down from time to time, and there are some genuine jerks out there in our pews. But there are also the finest people I've ever known who genuinely care about God and about people. People like you and me. Please be patient. God isn't finished with any of us yet.

Answers to Prayer

I sometimes hear people say, "Well, God didn't answer my prayer." They are wrong. God always answers prayer . . . but not necessarily the way we want Him to. Here are four ways that God answers prayer:

• He says, "no!" As a loving Father, God knows that some things we want aren't good for us or for those around us. He simply shakes His celestial head and says, "No, my child." In these cases, it is no use arguing with God. His "no" is not only for today; it is for every tomorrow that will follow today.

• He says, "slow. The timing is not right." This is not "no." It's "not right now." God may want to bring other people into the situation or arrange circumstances so more people will benefit. Delay, however, is not a denial.

Timing makes a miracle. If you need $500 and you don't have any way to pay it and a check comes, then it's a miracle. If you have plenty of money and you get a check for $500, it's not a miracle. God is more concerned with our hearts than about a day, a week, or even years. He will orchestrate His answers so that we see His hand and His heart more clearly.

• He says, "grow." Many times the reason God wants us to wait is so He can work on our motives and our character. I believe God often delays His answers to purify our hearts. He wants us to grow strong in Him and His purposes.

• He says, "go!" We like that answer! God may also say, "go and. . . ." God speaks to our hearts and gives us the sense that He wants us to do something with His answer. He may want us to use the gift in a way we haven't considered before, or He may want us to tell others of His goodness.

No, slow, grow, and go. They are all answers to prayer.

How to Know God's Will

People often ask, "How can I know God's will?" I believe God's will is the compilation of the series of godly decisions you and I make every day. He leads us to honor Him, to be kind to someone, to walk away from sin, and to make a thousand other "little" decisions. As we make those, the "big" decisions become clearer and clearer. It is very difficult to determine God's will for our lives in the big issues if we aren't walking with Him in the small ones. As we walk with God, He will use several things to give us direction:

Scripture

The Bible is full of truth, admonitions, commands, and promises to give us clear direction. No, every truth about life is not found in the Bible. It doesn't tell us whether to buy a foreign or domestic car, but the principles about life transcend cultures and time. They are truths about human nature, relationships, motivation, and about the nature of God Himself. Become a student of the Scriptures. They contain a gold mine of truth!

Prayer

As we pray, and as godly people pray for us, the clouds of confusion and doubt slowly lift. Motives surface, we can confess sin, and our hearts are tuned to God's. In my experience, and in the experience of many others, the best way to position ourselves to hear a word from God is through the disciplines of prayer, fasting, and solitude.

Godly Advice

People who have trusted God for many years have a wisdom that is a fountain of insight for us. Be careful, though; just because someone is in a leadership position doesn't mean he or she is necessarily wise. I would hope that is the case, but we need to be wise in how we choose our counselors. If we choose wisely, we can draw on that person's rich storehouse of experience and insight.

Circumstances

Sometimes circumstances lead us down the wrong road. I asked a college student how she picked a particular school, and she said, "It was the first one to send me a letter of acceptance, so I said 'yes.'" Obstacles aren't necessarily God's roadblocks. They may be His way of saying, "Trust Me for the process as well as the product." If, however, you want to be a professional opera singer and no music school or group will have you, there just might be a message there for you! Pay attention!

Peace

There is a sense of rightness about the path God has chosen for us. It doesn't mean everything will go smoothly. That would be comfort, not peace. The struggle can be a wonderful catharsis for us to deepen our perception, strengthen our character, and learn the difference between peace and comfort.

In most cases, we won't trust God until we have to. We will trust in our own wisdom or the ideas of someone else until we fail so miserably we finally turn to God. And after all, what is God most interested in? Our success? No, He is most interested in us developing a deep, loving, trusting relationship with Him. He will put us in situations that force us to depend on Him.

Trust and Expectations

Paul wrote Timothy about the glories and the struggles of spiritual life. His two letters provide many insights about the discipline necessary to walk with God, as well as the incredible rewards. In his second letter, Paul wrote:

> Endure hardship with us like a good soldier of Christ Jesus. No one serving as a soldier gets involved in civilian affairs—he wants to please his commanding officer. Similarly, if anyone competes as an athlete, he does not receive the victor's crown unless he competes according to the rules. The hardworking farmer should be the first to receive a share of the crops. Reflect on what I am saying, for the Lord will give you insight into all this. (II Timothy 2:3-7)

Soldier, athlete, and farmer. Let's see how these metaphors relate to you and me.

• A soldier obeys his commanding officer. There are clear lines of authority for his provision and protection on the battlefield and in camp. The soldier may not understand everything that is going on, but the commander has a broader view. In the same way, God protects and provides for us. His wisdom is far above ours because He sees the entire scope of the battlefield of our lives. We can obey Him because He knows what He's doing, and He values our contribution to His cause.

• An athlete must compete according to the rules of the game. If he doesn't have integrity, he is disqualified. Years ago, Rosie Ruiz crossed the tape and won the Boston Marathon. The crowds cheered, but strange reports began to surface. It was discovered that she had ridden the subway from early in the race to near the finish line. No wonder she was so fresh at the end! Ruiz made a fool of herself and became a laughing stock and a target of jokes on late night television shows.

In 1989, the pop music group, Milli Vanilli, won a Grammy as "The Best New Artist." They had a #1 hit and the #1 album that year. Later the world learned that Milli Vanilli lip-synched the lyrics to their songs. When their lie was uncovered, the kids dropped them like a hot potato! They were nothing but a couple of fakes.

Emmanuel Ninger was a landscape artist. One day, he walked into his neighborhood grocery store, picked up some things, and paid with a crisp, new $20 bill. The lady at the cash register had been washing turnips. Her hands were wet, and when she touched the bill, the ink smeared. She called the police. They searched his apartment and found bills drying on his easel. Minger was arrested and sent to jail for forgery. Ironically, four of Ninger's landscapes were seized and sold for $16,000. He later said that it took as long to paint a $20 bill as to paint a landscape. Emmanuel Ninger was found to be nothing but a fraud, but he could have been so much more. The moral to this story is: It takes as much effort to do wrong as it does to do right—and it doesn't pay nearly as well.

What are the rules for you and me? How can we avoid being a fool, a fake, or a fraud? We can start with the Ten Commandments, and we can find guidelines and commands to guide us throughout the pages of Scripture. Jesus said, "A new command I give you: Love one another as I have loved you" (John 13:34). What would the world be like if even a fraction of us followed that rule? We have rules of ethical conduct in our vocations and professions that are important for us to follow, as well as guidelines of citizenship, such as paying taxes and obeying the speed limits. Our willingness to follow these is an indication of our commitment to authority in our lives. We will be rewarded in many ways for "playing according to the rules."

• A farmer receives rewards for his hard work. He plows, plants, weeds, and waters, and eventually his harvest is 30-, 60-, or 100-fold. His family and his community rejoice when the crop is harvested, and they all benefit from his labors.

I've known some people who felt guilty for reaping such a large harvest. God has blessed them, but they can't enjoy it. I try to encourage them to do two things: Give thanks and give to others. There is nothing wrong with wealth, as long as *we* own it and *it* doesn't own us. One of the surest ways to know if we own it is to give significant portions of it away.

All three—the soldier, the athlete, and the farmer—exhibit a clear commitment to their goals and the discipline to see it through to completion. We might conclude that ethical obedience yields rewards.

All of the North Star Principles are important, but developing spiritual strength gives meaning and direction to every goal, every activity, and every relationship. We will be wise to make this principle our highest priority.

❑ Describe the times when you have felt closest to God.

❑ In what ways is God's wisdom goal-oriented? In what ways is it people-oriented?

❑ Reflect on Elijah's experience near the stream. Do you usually blame God for difficulties or see them as learning opportunities? Explain:

❑ How have you seen obvious examples of God's power?

❑ How have you noticed subtle examples?

❏ In what ways do you need God's power in your life today?

❏ Have you done things for which you don't feel forgiven? Explain:

❏ How would being convinced that you are completely forgiven by God change your life?

❏ Do you need to make restitution for anything?

❏ Who among God's people have encouraged you most?

❏ Have "God's people let you down"? Explain:

❑ Have you noticed each of the four possible answers to prayer—no, slow, grow, and go—in your experience? Give examples:

❑ Which of the factors in discovering God's will are you actively pursuing? Which are you neglecting? Explain:

❑ What are some of the rewards of obeying the commander, competing according to the rules, and working hard to grow spiritual crops?

❏ Complete these statements:
The state of my spiritual life today is (strengths and weaknesses, hopes and hurts):

Lord, I want . . .

14
SET YOUR HEADING

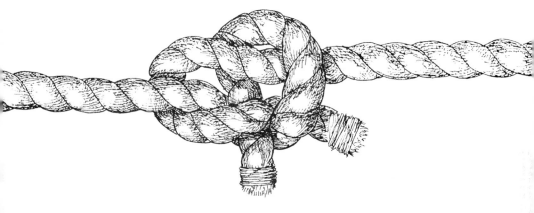

We have examined and refined our sense of purpose. We looked at the important contribution our backgrounds and personalities make in our direction and willingness to take risks. We have identified priorities, and we have found some obstacles which often block our paths to success. At this point in our journey, we need to get out our maps and set the heading on a definite course. This is the detailed plan. Some of us are stimulated by glowing generalities, but we become bored or frustrated when it comes to specifics. Others of us love the specifics, but we need a clearer vision of the overall direction so the specifics are in context. A detailed analysis without knowing where we are going isn't worth much.

Without a schedule and a budget, we don't have a plan. Planning is difficult but necessary work. Great dreams can die for lack of planning. It is here that many of our hopes and desires either come to life or are abandoned. We need a battlefield mentality. We have foes to fight and champions to defeat.

There's a price to be paid in planning. Years ago, I realized that I pay either on the front end or the back end. I either pay for my decision in time by preparing well before I take a step, or I pay for it in doubt by wondering if I've made a bad choice when difficulties come. The planning and preparation process determines my confidence level in my decisions. If I have made a quick decision, I am much quicker to doubt that decision when difficulties come. But if I have gone through the process of analysis and reflection, if I have genuinely sought God on the matter, and if I have wanted what is best for others, not just for myself, then the struggles usually are not devastating. In fact, if I'm sure of my direction, I sometimes even welcome the difficulties as challenges to be conquered. Attitude makes all the difference, but attitude is shaped by preparation.

Struggle has great value. It gives us perspective, and it deepens us. If we realize our difficulties have resulted from impulsive decisions, we learn to be more patient and reflective next time. We learn this important lesson by paying the high price of failure or confusion today.

Assessing Priorities

Some of us have listed 673 high priorities in this book. That's ambitious. It's also probably not very wise. The fewer goals we have, the greater our focus can be—and the likelihood of success is much higher. How do you decide which priorities to focus on first? Good question! I would guess that:

- Missouris will pick the hardest ones first.
- Paradise Stars will pick the easiest.
- Intrepids will pick the ones that are safest.
- Calypsos will choose the ones that offer the most systematic approach and measurable results.

There's absolutely nothing wrong with these choices. Each personality has its own comfort level with risk. The way I prioritize is by thinking of the Pareto Principle, the 80-20 rule. It means:

- You get 80% of your work done in 20% of your time.
- 20% of the salesmen sell 80% of the products.
- 20% of the fishermen catch 80% of the fish.
- 20% of the people at a picnic eat 80% of the food. (So figure out who those 20% are and don't invite them. You'll save money on groceries!)

Important questions about priorities and planning are: Which ones will kickstart others? Which are dependent on others? Are there patterns in which one priority either augments the success or resists the fulfillment of another?

For those in mid-life, author Gail Sheehy asks several penetrating questions which help crystallize our priorities:

- Are you preparing to meet the crossroads of midlife?
- Are you ready to search for a new direction leading to more meaning?
- How do you plan to prolong your physical health?
- Do you know how to maintain your sexual potency?
- What things can you do to nourish your spirit?
- Are you willing to risk deeper intimacy that will offer you a buffer against the inevitable losses of middle and later life?[1]

A Word about Divorce

The tremendous accumulation of stresses of background, career, poor communication and unrealistic expectations all collapse on that most important and most vulnerable relationship—marriage. All couples have problems. Some, however, won't or can't resolve their problems effectively. The changes at mid-life seem to bring greater pressures on this relationship than any other time because children are leaving home, careers are in transition, and people are actively assessing their futures. This book is not designed to be a treatise on marriage counseling, but I would be in error if I didn't address this important topic. If your marriage is rocky, please consider these suggestions:

• Find a competent marriage counselor who can help you rebuild trust and sort out expectations. Talk to your pastor or ask friends who have gone to a good counselor for a referral.

• If you are seriously contemplating a divorce, first attend a divorce recovery support group. Many people live with such relational stress that they easily acquire a "grass-is-greener" mentality. Attending a divorce recovery support group will give you a more accurate perspective of what people experience when they divorce. The experience may motivate you to try harder to save your marriage. A divorce is almost never the end of your problems. It only swaps one set of difficulties for another set—often a bigger and more complicated set.

• Act responsibly during times of stress in your marriage. Don't consider—or dive into—other romantic relationships when things at home aren't going well. Have the courage and integrity to remain pure so that there aren't far bigger problems in an already rocky relationship. If you have already made big mistakes, repent of the wrongs and get help.

• Always seek safety if there is physical violence, and especially, protect your children from any violence or genuine threats of violence.

• Try as hard as you can as long as you can to honor the commitment of marriage. Many people feel a great sense of relief immediately after they leave their spouse, but that relief is often replaced soon after with heartache. You can't make the other person in the relationship respond. All you can do is all you can do, but be sure you have exhausted every means of reconciliation. You will be glad you did.

Doing What's Right

We will be wise to evaluate our definition of success from time to time. Too many of us think we are doing well when our salary or position compares favorably to someone else's. But life is far more than positions, possessions, and prestige. As we set our heading, we need to consider what is right, not what gets us a notch higher on some arbitrary pecking order. Golda Meir, Prime Minister of Israel during the turbulent years of war between 1969 and 1974, stated, "I can honestly say that I was never affected by the question of the success of an undertaking. If I felt it was the right thing to do, I was for it regardless of the possible outcome." Meir's purpose transcended normal definitions of success. Ours should, too.

Planning and Timing

The next exercise gives you the opportunity to determine which goals are your highest priorities. You can then begin to plan effectively. In this plan you can consider what strengths you bring, from what outside resources you can enlist help, the particular needs you will have in reaching your goal, the obstacles you must overcome, the price you will have to pay, and the steps of implementation (including the schedule and the budget).

❏ Review chapters 8 and 10. List the dreams and priorities you wrote there.

❏ Which of your priorities will be stepping stones to help you accomplish other ones? Which will hinder the attaining of others?

❏ How does your personality shape your choices?

❏ Determine which choices are most important to focus on first. (How are you determining these priorities?)

❑ Priority #1:

Clearly define what you want to happen. (What does success look like?)

Identify strengths which will help you accomplish this goal.

Identify your needs (accountability, focus, money, time, etc.).

Identify outside resources which can assist you.

Identify obstacles which might hinder you (people, fear, expertise, etc.).

Identify the costs you will have to pay to accomplish your goal.

Identify specific steps, schedule, and budget (in time and money).

❏ Priority #2:

Clearly define what you want to happen. (What does success look like?)

Identify strengths which will help you accomplish this goal.

Identify your needs (accountability, focus, money, time, etc.).

Identify outside resources which can assist you.

Identify obstacles which might hinder you (people, fear, expertise, etc.).

Identify the costs you will have to pay to accomplish your goal.

Identify specific steps, schedule, and budget (in time and money).

❑ Priority #3:
Clearly define what you want to happen. (What does success look like?)

Identify strengths which will help you accomplish this goal.

Identify your needs (accountability, focus, money, time, etc.).

Identify outside resources which can assist you.

Identify obstacles which might hinder you (people, fear, expertise, etc.).

Identify the costs you will have to pay to accomplish your goal.

Identify specific steps, schedule, and budget (in time and money).

❏ Priority #4:
Clearly define what you want to happen. (What does success look like?)

Identify strengths which will help you accomplish this goal.

Identify your needs (accountability, focus, money, time, etc.).

Identify outside resources which can assist you.

Identify obstacles which might hinder you (people, fear, expertise, etc.).

Identify the costs you will have to pay to accomplish your goal.

Identify specific steps, schedule, and budget (in time and money).

❏ Priority #5:
Clearly define what you want to happen. (What does success look like?)

Identify strengths which will help you accomplish this goal.

Identify your needs (accountability, focus, money, time, etc.).

Identify outside resources which can assist you.

Identify obstacles which might hinder you (people, fear, expertise, etc.).

Identify the costs you will have to pay to accomplish your goal.

Identify specific steps, schedule, and budget (in time and money).

❏ How do you know how many priorities you can handle at one time?

❏ How do you know when to move on to tackle another one?

❏ How do you know when to reassess a particular priority and redirect your efforts?

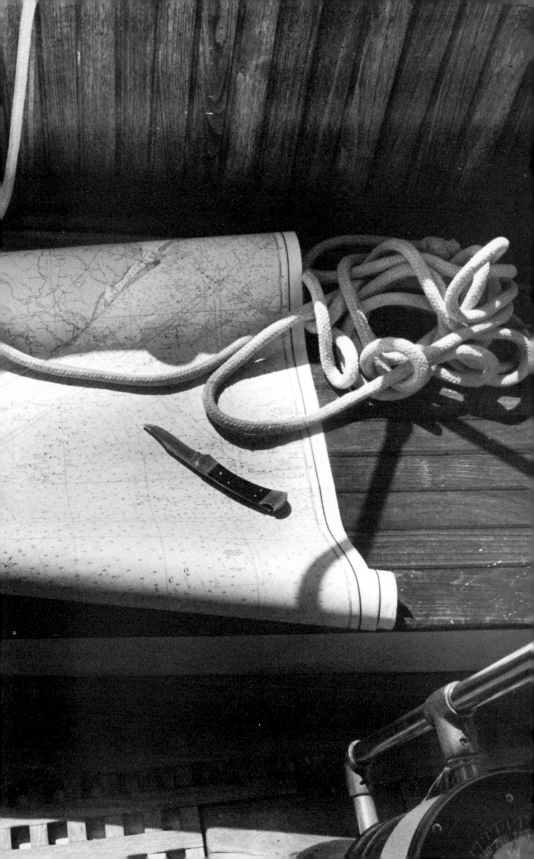

15
CHECK YOUR COURSE

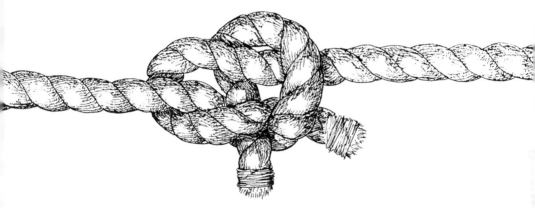

A good navigator checks his position and heading from time to time to be sure he hasn't drifted off course. In the old days, sailors used a sextant to "shoot" the sun and stars to get an accurate reading. Today, they use LORAN satellite instrumentation to identify their exact position within a few feet. We all have landmarks in our lives: the gas station where we turn to go home, the smile on our child's face to let us know she's happy, the affirmation of a boss who appreciates a job well done. Each priority and specific plan has its own landmarks to let us know if we are getting where we wanted to go—relationally, financially, emotionally, or vocationally.

Chapter 2 identified the landmarks of discontent—evidences of death by inches. We may have been "dead in the water," or we may have been in the way of a tsunami, a tidal wave of a life out of control! Or perhaps we were making progress—but in a direction we didn't want to go. The landmarks of progress are different for each of us, but they are clear and unmistakable. Here are some landmarks we can look for as we discover our North Stars and pursue them with all our hearts:

A Sense of Satisfaction

As we pursue our hearts' dreams, the journey will be full of satisfaction and fulfillment. We will have an abiding peace—even when we encounter obstacles—because we know we're going in the right direction and our lives count for something much bigger than ourselves.

A Heightened Awareness and Alertness

A friend told me, "When I paint, I notice far more colors in everything I see. My eyes are more alive." When we are on course for our North Star, we are more perceptive about people, obstacles, and opportunities around us.

Looking Forward to Each Day

Instead of dreading another boring day, we eagerly anticipate another step toward our goal and the amazing journey along the way.

Rich Relationships

Instead of using people, we love them. Instead of wearing masks and playing roles, we are honest. Instead of trying to change people to suit us, we can affirm them for who they really are. We will see the good in people instead of criticizing them for not fitting into our mold of demands and expectations.

Creativity

As we feel comfortable in our areas of strength and in the pursuit of our North Star, our creativity level will soar. That doesn't mean, of course, that we will all be creative in the same ways. Some are artistic, and some create new systems. Some find new ways to help people, and some take charge in fresh ways that stimulate others.

Passion

The old apathy and cynicism will fade as we have a new, gripping zeal to accomplish new goals. Our eyes will show this passion, and our minds will be filled with desire for others to share the thrill of our pursuit.

Adventure

As our confidence grows, we will be willing to take new steps of risk in goals and relationships. These steps may succeed or fail, but we are secure in our identities. Life becomes a great adventure!

Energy

Determining our North Star can produce a teenager's energy level in an old codger! A renewed zest for life shapes every interaction and every moment of our day. Sure, we'll need to rest from time to time, but we will look forward to taking the next step.

Surprises and Magnets

As we tap into the spiritual realm, our goals line up with God's purposes, and He works in surprising ways. Increasingly, we learn to look for the hand of God in everything we do, and quite often, we sense His gracious presence. He brings people and resources together to meet needs and fulfill His promises.

A Sense of Rightness

There is something wonderfully peaceful in knowing we are doing the will of God. Things may not go perfectly smoothly and, in fact, we may experience turmoil because our God-inspired integrity conflicts with others, but we have a feeling that we are on the right track . . . God's track.

Guilt Relief

Being on God's track means we know we are forgiven for our wrongs and we forgive others who hurt us. Our lives are no longer colored by guilt, bitterness, and the desire for revenge.

Honesty

We are honest with ourselves about our own choices. We also learn when and how to be honest with others to restore and encourage them.

Thankfulness

One of the most attractive qualities in anyone's life is thankfulness. A genuine heart of appreciation for God and for people lightens our hearts and makes us fun to be around.

Some of the landmarks are measurable. For example, we reach a certain goal in our 401(k) or another investment, we are promoted to a desired position in the company, or we shoot under 80 at our favorite golf course (or under 100!). Calypsos love the tangible, measurable goals, but many goals that are most precious to us are intangible: love, intimacy, encouragement, and forgiveness. We learn to measure the ones that are indeed measurable without devaluing those that can't be quantified.

❏ List your top priorities (five to ten of them). What are several landmarks for each one which will tell you if you are on course? (For each priority, you might have some measurable landmarks and some that are not measurable.)

❏ What are the indications that you are on course pursuing your North Star?

❏ Look at the list of landmarks in this chapter. Which of these are you experiencing now?

Which do you really want to experience? Explain:

❏ What mid-course corrections do you need to make?

❑ How will you make each mid-course correction? When? With whom?

How to Keep your Dream Alive though the Detours, Darkness, and Dungeons

As I mentioned earlier, I'm convinced that a genuine, God-given dream goes through a cycle of birth, death, and rebirth. In almost every walk of life we hear stories of men and women who had a clear vision, but through tragic or confusing circumstances, that vision died. Sometime later, often in surprising, serendipitous ways, the vision was reborn and fulfilled. No matter how clear our dream might be, we can expect some detours, darkness, and even a dungeon or two where our dream—and our heart—is imprisoned. One of my favorite stories about this cycle is the saga of Joseph.

Joseph was the 11th son of Jacob. He was the first child of Jacob's beloved wife, Rachel, and that made him the apple of his father's eye. Jacob gave Joseph a beautiful, multi-colored coat. His brothers had only goat skins and plain cloth. They were jealous of the coat, but much more jealous of their father's attention. They hated their favored brother.

When he was 17 years old, Joseph had a couple of dreams. In Genesis we read:

> Joseph had a dream, and when he told it to his brothers, they hated him all the more. He said to them, "Listen to this dream I had: We were binding sheaves of grain out in the field when suddenly my sheaf rose and stood upright, while your sheaves gathered around mine and bowed down to it."
>
> His brothers said to him, "Do you intend to reign over us? Will you actually rule us?" And they hated him all the more because of his dream and what he had said.
>
> Then he had another dream, and he told it to his brothers. "Listen," he said, "I had another dream, and this time the sun and moon and eleven stars were bowing down to me."
>
> When he told his father as well as his brothers, his father rebuked him and said, "What is this dream you had? Will your mother and I and your brothers actually come and bow down to the ground before you?" His brothers were jealous of him, but his father kept the matter in mind. (Genesis 37:5-11)

Who gave Joseph those dreams? God did. But God didn't tell him to tell his hateful brothers! That was really dumb! But even that was a part of God's design. (One lesson we learn is to be very careful about choosing the people to whom we entrust our deepest dreams.)

Some time later, Joseph's brothers were tending sheep far from home. Jacob sent Joseph to check on them. (That was really going to help his standing with his brothers!)

They saw Joseph at a distance. They knew it was him because they recognized his colorful coat. They sneered, "Here comes that dreamer!" As he walked up, the brothers devised a plan. They would kill him and throw him into a pit. They planned to tell their father that a wild animal had killed him. The oldest brother, Reuben, wanted to save his young brother. He convinced his brothers to throw Joseph into the pit but not to kill him. Reuben planned to secretly go back to get Joseph and return him to his father. So they grabbed Joseph, took his coat from him, and threw him into the empty cistern. Undoubtedly, Joseph thought Reuben's plan gave him a way out. He may have thought, "Maybe the dream can still be fulfilled if things are like they were before . . . ," but God had other plans.

While Reuben was gone, the brothers saw a caravan heading toward Egypt. They sold Joseph to the traders. Reuben returned, but his brothers told him what they had done. They dipped the coat in goat's blood and took it to Jacob. Their father grieved bitterly over his beloved son's supposed death.

In Egypt, Joseph was sold to Potiphar, one of Pharaoh's officials. In everything Joseph did, he prospered. Potiphar's wife, however, had ideas for Joseph that went somewhat beyond washing dishes and sweeping the patio. She ripped his clothes off him, but he ran away. She then played the rape card, and Joseph was thrown into prison.

If I had been Joseph, I would be thinking, *Hey, God, You gave me those dreams! Look at me now. My own brothers sold me into slavery. I did what was right with Potiphar's wife. I didn't have sex with her, but her lies landed me in jail. What's the deal?* But we hear no words of protest from Joseph. Over and over again, we read, "And God was with Joseph."

We don't know exactly how long Joseph was in prison. It was many years. One day the Pharaoh's baker and cupbearer were thrown into prison. That night, each of them had a dream. When they related their dreams to the other prisoners, Joseph stepped forward to interpret them. Joseph told them the cupbearer would be restored to his position, but the baker would be executed. That's exactly what happened. Joseph pleaded to the cupbearer, "Don't forget me!" But the cupbearer didn't mention Joseph for two long years. If I'd been Joseph, I'd have been really upset! I interpreted a dream for a guy, and the thanks I get is to be forgotten! Those must have been dark times in his life, but the Bible gives no indication of any discouragement. It only says, "And God was with Joseph."

This is God's way of reminding us that prevailing, negative circumstances are no indication that God has abandoned us. God may be silent on the surface, but He is still active behind the scenes.

At a later date, the Pharaoh had disturbing dreams. None of his magicians or wise men could interpret them. Finally, the cupbearer remembered Joseph! He told the Pharaoh about the prisoner interpreting his dream so long ago in the darkness of the dungeon, so the Pharaoh called for Joseph. After a quick shower and a shave, Joseph, the accused rapist, stood before the ruler of the greatest country in the world. The Pharaoh said to him, "I had a dream, and no one can interpret it. But I have heard it said of you that when you hear a dream you can interpret it."

If I had been Joseph—after years of being abused by my brothers, sold into slavery, accused falsely by Potiphar's wife, and forgotten in the dungeon for many years, I would have said, "You bet, Pharaoh, baby! I'm your man!"

But Joseph didn't. He calmly stated to Pharaoh, "I cannot do it, but God will give Pharaoh the answer he desires." The ruler related his dreams, and God spoke to the attentive Joseph, who gave the interpretation to Pharaoh.

The dual dreams were of seven years of plenty followed by seven years of famine. The Pharaoh was so impressed with Joseph that he made him Prime Minister over all of Egypt, the #2 man in the entire kingdom! Joseph, now a wise administrator, stored grain in the years of plenty to have enough for the days of famine.

A dream got Joseph into trouble. A dream got him out. And a dream kept him going.

About 10 years later, in the midst of the severe famine which plagued that part of the globe, Jacob's family cupboard was empty. The old man sent 10 of his sons down to Egypt because he heard they had grain stored there. The brothers came and bowed before the Prime Minister (remember the dream?) to ask if they could buy food. Through a series of tests, Joseph determined that his brothers had repented of their sin against him. Finally, he revealed himself to his astonished brothers.

> His brothers then came and threw themselves down before him. "We are your slaves," they said.
>
> But Joseph said to them, "Don't be afraid. Am I in the place of God? You intended it to harm me, but God intended it for good to accomplish what is now being done, the saving of many lives." (Genesis 50:18-20)

What sustained Joseph through the detour of slavery, the darkness of not seeing his dream fulfilled, and his years in the dungeon? He believed that somehow God had a purpose in it all. I don't think he could have articulated how that purpose would be worked out, but he never doubted that God is real, and God has a purpose. He trusted that his God-given dream would be fulfilled. In his wildest imagination, I don't think he would have pictured himself as Prime Minister of Egypt and in the position to save his father and his entire family from starvation, but that was God's incredible plan.

Think of how differently things would have turned out if Joseph had given in to temptation and had sex with Potiphar's wife. I suspect he would have been executed instead of jailed. And what would have happened if Joseph had given up on God when the baker and cupbearer were suddenly thrown into prison? Joseph wouldn't have interpreted the dreams, and the cupbearer wouldn't have given a good report about him later. And what would have happened if after years of unfair imprisonment Joseph was really angry when he was ushered into Pharaoh's presence and complained about the harsh treatment and unfair sentence instead of looking to God for guidance? And what would have happened if, out of the desire for revenge, Joseph had refused his brothers the grain their family needed to survive? Joseph had a lot of occasions when he could have given up on God and his dream. But he didn't. His circumstances seemed to take Joseph downhill, but in fact, he was on the fast track to success!

How many times do we gripe and complain and grumble when things don't work out the way we hoped? Some of us must think cynicism is an Olympic competition—and we plan to win the gold! Instead of instantly reacting by griping and asking "Why?" it would be far more productive to respond, "Lord, what do You want me to learn here? How is this a part of Your plan?" And even if God doesn't let us in on any secrets, we can be certain that He does, indeed, have a plan, and that plan is a good one. When your "why's" turn into "what now's," you are moving toward spiritual maturity and strength.

❑ Describe some of your experiences which exemplify the "birth-death-rebirth" cycle of a dream.

❑ Describe in your own words what you think Joseph's perspective was in the dark hours of the dungeon. What might he have been thinking? What might he have been feeling?

❑ Has griping, cynicism, and complaining cost you anything? Explain:

❑ What can you do today to develop in your own life Joseph's attitude of trusting God no matter what?

❑ What differences will that attitude make in your life (goals, motivations, relationships, etc.)?

The North Star Principles, Revisited

Throughout this book, we have examined how we can apply the North Star Principles in every aspect of our lives. Their value doesn't end, however, when our priorities are determined and our course is set. These principles continue to guide our motivations, correct our missteps, and keep us on course for success and significance.

We all need reminders from time to time. Formulate a strategy to help you stay focused on and apply the North Star Principles. You might want to:

—memorize them and repeat them every day,

—teach them to your co-workers,

—talk about them with your family,

—teach them in a class,

—make them into a screen saver on your computer,

—find a picture which symbolizes each one and put these around your office or home, or

—use the companion *North Star Journal* to reinforce these principles in your life.

❑ What specific, creative, personal steps can you take to reinforce the North Star Principles in your life?

❏ How has your study and reflection in this book helped you make progress in each of the principles? (Consider: How have the principles been clarified in your thoughts? How have you risen to the challenges to apply them?)

—Embrace risk as a way of life.

—Take responsibility.

—Be honest about your emotions.

—Never stop learning.

—Value meaningful relationships.

—Develop spiritual strength.

—See life as an adventure!

EPILOGUE
NO RETREAT—NO REGRETS

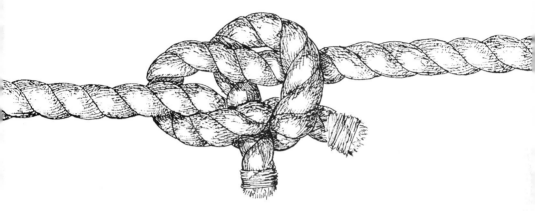

Teddy Stallard was a pathetic little kid. He was dirty, his clothes were a mess, and his hair matted to his head. His expression in school day after day was a deadpanned stare. His teacher, Miss Thompson, tried to communicate with the boy, but he always mumbled one-word answers. It was hard for her to see even the slightest potential in this rumpled, emotionless, unmotivated little boy. She said she loved everybody in her class, but over the months, her attention—and her affection—drifted away from Teddy.

When Miss Thompson graded papers, she got a perverse joy marking Teddy's multitude of wrong answers and putting F's on his papers. She should have seen all this coming. His school records read:

1st Grade: Teddy shows promise with his work and attitude, but poor home situation.

2nd Grade: Teddy could do better. Mother is seriously ill. He receives little help at home.

3rd Grade: Teddy is a good boy but too serious. He is a slow learner. His mother died this year.

4th Grade: Teddy is very slow, but well-behaved. His father shows no interest.

Christmas came to Miss Thompson's fifth grade class, and the children brought her a blizzard of presents. They crowded around her desk to watch her open them. After several packages and many ooohs and ahhhhs, she picked up the one from Teddy. The others were nicely wrapped in colorful Christmas paper. Teddy's was in paper from a grocery bag. On the paper was written simply, "For Miss Thompson from Teddy." She opened the gift, and a gaudy rhinestone bracelet fell out. Half the stones were missing. Also in the box was a bottle of cheap perfume.

The other children poked each other and giggled at the sight of Teddy's gift, but Miss Thompson quieted them by putting on the bracelet and rubbing drops of perfume on her wrists and giving the girls a sniff. "Doesn't it smell lovely?" They agreed it did.

After the last bell rang that day and the class dismissed, Teddy lingered behind. Slowly . . . very slowly . . . he made his way to Miss Thompson's desk. He murmured, "Miss Thompson, you smell just like my mother . . . and her bracelet looks real pretty on you, too. I'm glad you like my presents." When Teddy left the room, Miss Thompson got down on her knees and wept. She asked God to forgive her for being so cold and calloused to that poor, little boy.

When the children came to class the next day, they had a new teacher. It was Miss Thompson's body, all right, but inside was a changed woman. She committed herself to looking beyond the outside of children and peering into their hearts. She was determined to love them in a way that would make a difference in their lives—especially the slow, shy, or wounded ones, and especially Teddy Stallard.

The months passed and summer vacation was only a few days away. The Spring had seen Teddy make remarkable progress in the class—and in his confidence.

He had begun the year several grade levels behind the other students, but now he had caught up.

The summer came, and in the Fall, Miss Thompson had a new class. The years passed, but she didn't forget about Teddy. One day she received a note:

> Dear Miss Thompson,
>   I wanted you to be the first to know. I will be graduating second in my class.
>   Love,
>   Teddy Stallard

After four more years, another letter came:

> Dear Miss Thompson,
>   They just told me I will be graduating first in my class. I wanted you to be the first to know. The university has not been easy, but I liked it.
>   Love,
>   Teddy Stallard

And four years later,

> Dear Miss Thompson,
>   As of today, I am Theodore Stallard, M.D. How about that? I wanted you to be the first to know. I am getting married next month, the 27th to be exact. I want you to come and sit where my mother would sit if she were alive. You are the only family I have now. Dad died last year.
>   Love,
>   Teddy Stallard

A few weeks later, Miss Thompson was escorted down the aisle and sat in Teddy's mother's seat at his wedding. It was a fitting request from someone whose life was forever changed by a loving teacher, and it was a fitting response from someone whose life was forever changed by a needy, loving child.[1]

Perhaps you identify today with Teddy Stallard. You see little potential in yourself. You feel lost and alone. Failures and shame seem to multiply and consume your life, and you need to take a step—even one—toward someone who can show you love and direction.

Or perhaps you identify with Miss Thompson. You have worked hard and well, but your heart is a bit cold. Reaching out to help someone else can be the beginning of a sequence of loving events that will change others' lives—and your own.

It is important that we start well. It is more important that we finish well. One of the things we realize when we analyze our goals, dreams, and desires is that we can get off track very easily. We can become lethargic or bitter or compulsive in our work, but these only lead to heartache, not a rich, meaningful life. Remember Peter Lynch's words, "I don't know anyone who wished on his deathbed that he had spent more time at the office." People on their deathbeds lament a wasted life and the bitterness that drove a wedge between themselves and others.

I want to look back without regret. The decisions I make today are chiseling the epitaph on my tombstone, and I want those decisions to write beautiful words, not words of emptiness and bitterness.

Some of us are very happy about the words that are being carved in our lives every day, but many of us aren't. God is a God of second chances. Through His forgiveness and grace, we can start fresh each day. No matter how big our mistakes have been, we can make new decisions, chart different courses, and get to new destinations. If we have been blown far off course, the struggle to get back to the right course may be difficult and protracted, and we may always carry some of the scars of being off course for a while. But nothing is so important as valuing the right things and leaving a legacy of hope and love to those we care about.

I hope this book has been encouraging and enlightening to you. In conclusion, I invite you to anticipate the epitaph that you want written on your tombstone by your life's contribution.

❏ Think long and hard about what you want your epitaph to be. Consider the contribution you want to make and the legacy you want to leave behind. Write your epitaph on the tombstone under your name.

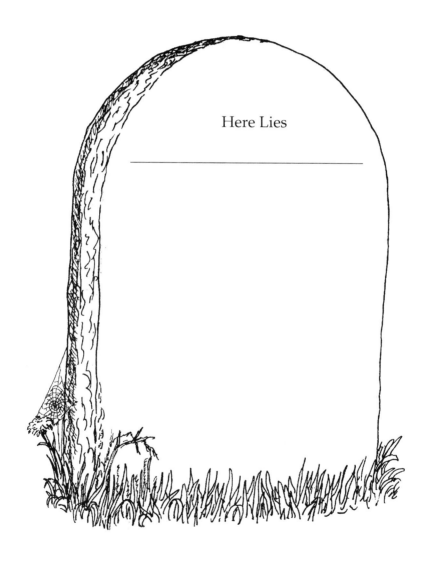

Here Lies

_____

NOTES

Chapter 2

1   Donald Phillips, *Lincoln on Leadership*, (Warner Books, New York, 1992), pp. 55-56.

Chapter 4

1   Erik Erikson, *Childhood and Society*, (New York: Norton, 1963)

2   Dr. Gary Collins, *Christian Counseling*, (Word, Dallas, 1988), p. 200.

3   Gail Sheehy, *Understanding Men's Passages*, (Random House, New York, 1998)

Chapter 6

1   Carl E. Wahlstrom, *Abraham Lincoln: Servant of the People,* (Achille J. St. Onge, Worcester, 1942), p. 19.

2   Adapted from Brian Tracy, *Maximum Achievement*, (Simon & Schuster, New York, 1993), pp. 147-148.

Chapter 11

1   Story adapted from an article in *The Baptist Standard*.

Chapter 14

1   Sheehy, Ibid.

Epilogue

1   Adapted from Charles Swindoll, *Hand Me Another Brick,* (Multnomah Press, Portland, Oregon), pp. 177-181.

QUOTES

Cut these out and put them on your mirror or computer.

• "The story of the human race is men and women selling themselves short." Abraham Maslow

• "A man's got to know his limitations." Dirty Harry

• "Without vision, the people perish." King Solomon

• Everything has a price tag. Every step forward takes time, energy, and it may require the effort of helping others understand. The price of success can be high, but the cost of stagnation is even higher.

• "I've learned that success is to be measured not so much by the position that one has reached in life as by the obstacles which one has overcome while trying to succeed." Booker T. Washington

• "Never give in. Never give in. Never, never, never, never —in nothing great or small, large or petty—never give in except to convictions of honor and good sense." Winston Churchill

• "We live life going forward, but we understand it looking backward." Soren Kirkegaard

• "If you ever have it all under control, you aren't really racing." Mario Andretti

• My dreams have been forged on the anvil of disappointment, and they have taken flight on the wings of successes and encouragement.

• Failure isn't the problem—it's how we interpret it. There's a world of difference between "I failed" and "I am a failure."

• "A man can do only what he can do. But if he does that each day, he can sleep at night and do it again the next day." Philosopher, humanitarian, and physician, Albert Schweitzer

• "When I examine myself and my methods of thought, I come to the conclusion that the gift of fantasy has meant more to me than my talent for absorbing positive knowledge." Albert Einstein

• "Security is mostly a superstition. It does not exist in nature, nor do the children of men as a whole experience it. Avoiding danger is no safer in the long run than outright exposure. Life is either a daring adventure or nothing." Helen Keller

• "God may allow His servant to succeed when He has disciplined him to a point where he does not need to succeed to be happy. The man who is elated by success and is cast down by failure is still a carnal man. At best his fruit will have a worm in it." A. W. Tozer

• "There's so much bad in the best of us and so much good in worst of us that it hardly behooves any of us to talk about the rest of us." My mother

• "Success is neither fame, wealth, nor power; rather it is seeking, knowing, loving and obeying God. If you seek, you will know; if you know, you will love; if you love, you will obey." Former Secretary General of the United Nations, Charles Malik

• "Funny things happen to those people who refuse to quit."

• "No man is worth his salt who is not ready at all times to risk his body, to risk his well-being, to risk his life, in a great cause." Teddy Roosevelt

• "When I stood naked before the guards, feeling ridiculous, I thought, *They cannot make me hate them.* As long as I can choose my attitude, they don't control me."
Victor Frankl

• "The last human freedom is our ability to choose our attitude in any set of circumstances." Victor Frankl

• "Real power is in the hands of the learning, not the learned." Ira Blumenthal

• "There is no pit so deep that God is not deeper still."
Corrie ten Boom

• Every day can be a great adventure if we open our eyes to the challenges and serendipitous opportunities He lays before us. Take advantage of them. Make your life count. Leave a lasting legacy. God uses the ordinary to do extraordinary things. That's the real North Star—living beyond yourself.

• "To put the world right in order, we must first put the nation in order; to put the nation in order, we must first put the family in order; to put the family in order, we must first cultivate our personal life; we must first set our hearts right." Confucius

• "Do you want to spend the rest of your life selling sugared water, or do you want to change the world?" Steve Jobs

• "True success is finding what God wants you to do and then doing it with all your heart."

• "If I had only known! If I had only known!" Thomas Carlyle

• Our last moments on earth will not be filled with regrets about unfinished goals, but with unshared love. Make a commitment to communicate your love often.

• "Sooner or later we all sit down to a banquet of consequences." Robert Louis Stevenson

• "Those who do not know how to weep with their whole heart don't know how to laugh either." Golda Meir

• "I loved what I was doing, but I came to a conclusion, and so did some others: What in the hell are we doing this for? I don't know anyone who wished on his deathbed that he had spent more time at the office." Peter Lynch

• People live for encouragement, and they die without it.

• Without a schedule and a budget, you don't have a plan.

• "If any of you lacks wisdom, he should ask God, who gives generously to all without finding fault, and it will be given to him" (James 1:5).

• "He forgave us all our sins, having canceled the written code, with its regulations, that was against us and that stood opposed to us; he took it away, nailing it to the cross" (Colossians 2:13b-14).

• What sustained Joseph through the detour of slavery, the darkness of not seeing his dream fulfilled, and his years in the dungeon? He believed that somehow, God had a purpose in it all.

• "I can honestly say that I was never affected by the question of the success of an undertaking. If I felt it was the right thing to do, I was for it regardless of the possible outcome." Golda Meir

• Nothing is so important as valuing the right things and leaving a legacy of hope and love to those we care about.

ABOUT THE AUTHORS

Dwight "Ike" Reighard is pastor of NorthStar Church, one of the fastest growing churches in the nation, in Kennesaw, Georgia. In addition to his role as a pastor, he speaks on the topic of leadership across North America as a corporate trainer and a church growth expert. Dr. Reighard has spoken to the management of Delta Airlines, Chick-fil-A, BellSouth Telecommunications, and many other companies and organizations.

He received a B.A. in religion (Magna Cum Laude) from Mercer University, a Master of Divinity from Luther Rice Seminary, a Doctor of Ministry from Luther Rice, and an Honorary Doctor of Literature from Southern California Theological Seminary.

He served as president of the Georgia Baptist Convention and is currently on the boards of several universities and other organizations, such as Liberty University, Rapha Treatment Centers, Alpha Care, and Psychological Studies Institute at Georgia State.

Dr. Reighard and his wife, Robin, have two daughters, Abigail and Danielle, and reside in Powder Springs, Georgia.

Pat Springle and Ike Reighard have collaborated on several other projects, including *Treasures from the Dark*, the *Treasures from the Dark Video Series*, and *The North Star Journal*. Springle has an M.A. in counseling and was the senior vice president for Rapha Treatment Centers. He has authored or co-authored more than 20 books. He lives in Friendswood, Texas, with his wife, Joyce, and his children, Catherine and Taylor.

FOR MORE INFORMATION . . .

. . . about additional resources and scheduling events, contact us at:

> Quantum Leap Publishing
> 3114 Cherokee Street, Ste. 201
> Kennesaw, GA 30144
>
> Phone: (770) 792-9923
> Fax: (770) 792-9957
> On the web:
>   www.quantumproductions.com